YOUNG, SUCCESSFUL & MISERABLE.

A blueprint to getting unstuck and reclaiming your natural freedom.

Kevin Holt

Copyright © 2020 by Kevin Holt. All rights reserved.

Published by Journeyman Books – Baar, Switzerland.

ISBN: 978-3-907282-00-7 (paperback)

ISBN: 978-3-907282-01-4 (e-book)

ISBN: 978-3-907282-02-1 (audiobook)

The contents of this book are for informational purposes only. The content is not intended to be a substitute for personal, professional psychiatric or psychological advice, diagnosis or treatment. Always seek the advice of your medical professional or other qualified mental health practitioner with any questions you may have regarding a medical condition.

Interior design by Luca Padovani

Author photo by Kelly Hoeltschi

Cover design by Luca Padovani

To Marion

For inspiration in entirely unexpected ways

Acknowledgements

Tim Witting, for your invaluable friendship and feedback.
Jennifer Ferguson, for your continuous support throughout this creation.
Scott McHugh, for pushing me along.
Robert Walters, for getting me over the finish line.

Contents

I. Where You Are Now — 7

II. Quit Your Bitching — 34

III. Decide Where You Want to Go — 64

IV. The Journey Ahead — 125

I.
Where You Are Now

If this book has found itself within the grasp of your eager little fingers, it's likely that you're feeling "stuck".

You want more from life, but aren't sure how to go about it.

Maybe you're in a go-nowhere corporate job.

Or maybe your corporate job is taking you places, but you aren't excited about the direction or the destination.

Perhaps you are unhappy with the type of romantic partner that you seem to keep attracting into your life. Or your friendships and relationships with family are unsatisfying.

It could be that you are struggling financially and buried in debt.

Whatever your present challenge may be, you are not exactly living in joy. Things are okay, you think you are sort of happy sometimes, and you attempt to escape your reality by dulling your feelings: going out for drinks 4 nights a week, smoking pot all day, eating junk food, going shopping, binge watching Netflix, and spending a lot of time in bed on the weekends to "recover" from your week.

You aren't exactly jumping out of bed with excitement each morning.

You feel content to continue on as you are, knowing that it's not so bad. It could be worse…

It could be much, much worse.

But mostly, you are bored, disappointed, disillusioned, and feel like you aren't good enough for something better. This is your life, and you're slowly and sadly coming to terms with it.

I. Where You Are Now

You used to have big dreams. Maybe you still do. But they aren't being accomplished.

Your dreams slowly fade with the years and you resign yourself to the thought that they are for someone else, for another life.

If you relate to any of this, then read on because I have good news for you.

There IS a better life out there for you—one in which you can reach your fullest potential, and live the life you've always dreamed about.

And Now is the perfect moment to alter your course.

I once felt exactly as you do now.

I spent several years of my career in a high-flying corporate consulting role. I had everything I was supposed to have in a job: a six-figure salary, great pension plan, corporate phone and expense card, international business travel.

As a top performer, I was told that as long as I continued to deliver for clients, I would be on a fast promotion track. I might even "make Partner some day!"

This was the dream. It was everything you are taught to aspire to in business school.

At first it was exciting.

I had a great boss, good colleagues. The work was challenging and interesting.

But after the first couple of promotions, I became very unhappy.

I remember clearly the final performance talk I had with my manager, when he congratulated me on my most recent promotion.

He laid out my future for me. It was a bright future with the company, a road map with regular promotions and salary increases at predictable intervals. He showed me what the next 5 or 10 years would look like as a high level executive, overseeing a sizable outsourced delivery center in Poland, on a Swiss salary and benefits package.

I was supposed to be excited.

Instead, the idea that the next several years of my life were already planned out made me feel so...

Bored.

Still worse, it had slowly begun to dawn on me that this wasn't *my* dream. It was *someone else's* dream, and it was being sold to me so that my time and livelihood could make someone else wealthy.

Then I thought, what right did I have to complain? I was part of the 1% of the world. There must have been millions of people in the world who would have *killed* for the opportunity I had been given – the status, the "job security", the earnings prospects, and the power and responsibility that came with it.

So I slogged it out a bit longer.

I thought that there might be something wrong with my thinking or my attitude, so I examined these carefully. I tried to be grateful for everything I had, which helped a little, for a time.

However, as time went on, my feelings of boredom and dis-empowerment increased.

I began to notice that most of my colleagues seemed unhappy too. Even much of the leadership did.

It had become a true grind.

One day, as I was sitting at my desk, grinding through the incredibly tedious testing of some new piece of software that the company leadership had sold the world as our industry's equivalent of the next cure for cancer, I suddenly stopped what I was doing.

I stared at my screen for several long minutes, doing nothing.

I slowly looked around the office. At my colleagues around me, grinding through the slog of their own work.

Then I looked back at my computer screen.

And I began to cry softly.

I had become a slave.

I was in a golden prison: nice salary, the "glorious" prospect of the next promotion and the carrot on a stick of "making Partner someday".

I had no belief in what I was doing. I was making pretty good money, but for what? How was I making the world a better place? What was I even supposed to do with the upper 6-figure carrot at the end of the stick? I owned 3 pairs of pants, did not own a car, the idea of buying a home didn't particularly appeal to me, and I preferred Couchsurfing to staying in nice hotels.

I had to "clock in", had to "be there" according to someone else's idea of a work schedule.

My occasional early departure at 5 p.m. would be followed with disparaging comments: "What, are you working part time?"

Or worse – no comment at all, just silent backstabbing from colleagues over the internal office messenger about the guy who "doesn't have enough work – look at us, slaving away here until 7 or 8 p.m. and this guy leaves at 5!", oblivious to the directly causal relationship between their daylong gossip over messenger and the fact that they routinely had to work late.

I had to dress a certain way, behave and speak a certain way and about only select, appropriate "corporate friendly" topics.

I was told not to use smiley faces in emails to clients. I was even once told that I should reduce the number of exclamation points that I used when writing emails!!!!!!

Anytime I tried to let my natural joy or enthusiasm shine through, I was given the feedback that I should "tone it down".

Imagine that. My inner child – the main character in my life's story—was slowly being poisoned.

"Yes, well, it's company policy", they might say.

I can imagine the performance discussions:

> "Kevin seems very enthusiastic when communicating with clients. He doesn't seem to understand that 'professionalism' means being a flat, dull, same-suit-wearing carbon copy of everyone else, operating under our corporate-approved, low frequency 'grind it out' mentality. We urgently need to make this guy less interested and excited".

After those silent tears I shed that day, I finally realized that I needed to make a change before my inner child died forever. I ended up quitting a few months later.

After taking 3 months off, I took a job at another company in a similar industry. I figured maybe it was just the job.

But the new job was no different. In many ways it was worse – more hierarchical, more emphasis on mistakes over successes, more conformity

I. Where You Are Now

under the marketing umbrella of "embracing diversity" in terms of skin color, but not original thinking.

Though "disruption" is often encouraged on the surface or in a company's marketing, rebellious ideas and behavior – including the "novel" idea that all people are of equal value, regardless of what job title and salary may indicate – are slowly ground out of you.

You eventually accept the situation and continue to operate at that low level frequency–the mildly satisfied, mostly bored, steady paycheck, live-for-the-weekends-and-holidays lifestyle.

I. Where You Are Now

Company Culture

Most of these companies, though they claim they are "flat" and that management's doors are "always open", are still run using a top-down, command-and-control hierarchical structure.

They still run their shop with the old "carrot on a stick" model; if you keep your head down and stay in line and fearful, you may be rewarded with a bonus, promotion or a salary increase.

Just be a "good worker" and you'll do well. Be a good little boy or girl. Be obedient.

Make no mistake, most company leadership still employs fear as the primary way to keep its employees meek and in control. They expect your biggest motivator to be the fear of losing your job or missing out on that next promotion.

No matter how "open" a director or executive tells you that they are, deep down, many of them are enamored with the "power" and "authority" that comes with their position, and will demonstrate it in both subtle and overt ways.

I have seen it employed with shocking transparency.

I once overheard one senior partner say, "People are afraid of me, and I find it quite useful."

This same partner also once remarked that he had "eleven slaves working for him" as he walked out of the office to go home at 4 p.m. while asking his slaves to "make him some money".

At a different firm, I occasionally attended meetings with high-level executives. These higher-ups would often be ten or more minutes late for the meeting (and you were supposed to accept this, even though these were the same people who would typically make a snarky comment when you showed up just one minute late; nice double standard).

At one particular meeting in which the Chairman of the Board was due to arrive (and arrived late), the tension in the air was palpable as everyone waited in nervous silence.

The room stiffened with a collective, barely audible in-breath when the Chairman finally walked in. Everyone struggled to appear professional, composed, and yet sunk down in their seats, hoping to escape the Chairman's attention.

The Chairman, of course, must have sensed this, and he made no attempt to diffuse the tension. A simple smile and asking the room, "How are you all doing today?" would have achieved that. He remained serious and expressionless, allowing nervous tension to build, like an energetic vampire getting his fix.

How lonely he must be, I thought.

In still another meeting, I witnessed a colleague's fear manipulated quite blatantly.

We were in a group meeting with the lead partners of one of our service lines. I was there to present some data. A junior accountant, Marc, had to adjust some figures on an Excel spreadsheet we were all watching on the overhead screen.

One of the leaders asked him an impossible question. Marc was clearly struggling with the task of doing something numerically impossible and how to communicate this to his "superior".

So he stammered, looking flustered and flushing red, while he made sure he had his facts right, searching for a way to tell the bosses that their concept was flawed.

The leader picked up on his nervousness–"What's the matter, Marc? Are you stressed?" he laughed, viciously, before Marc could stammer out an explanation.

In the corporate world, your fear can and will be used to control and intimidate you.

Using a person's fear against them is a form of violence.

Another form of violence is formulating a wish as a command rather than a request. The difference between a request and a command is that a command comes with the implication of punishment for disobeying it.

This is what Marshall Rosenberg—founder of the practice of Non-Violent Communication—means when he calls corporations and other hierarchical institutions "domination structures".

The ego is like a gas of dominance that will seep into and fill any space it can find. In its quest to express its need for power and significance, the ego will quickly find its home in a structure that carries with it implicit threats for non-compliance.

In order for these structures to sustain themselves, its members need to be obedient and look to an authority for cues on how they should speak and behave.

In such a structure, it becomes difficult to connect with the human side of a person. Most corporate environments feel dehumanizing for this reason. From a leadership point of view, your wholeness, your complexity, your inner child is suppressed and distilled down to a specific job role, a function. You have a serial number (an employee ID). You are a headcount, a resource to be allocated, part of the production line. There are legal frameworks, acceptable behaviors and opinions, and so forth.

I. Where You Are Now

Your job may no longer be meeting your needs

The main reason you feel as bored and dis-empowered as you do is simple: your job _is no longer meeting your needs._

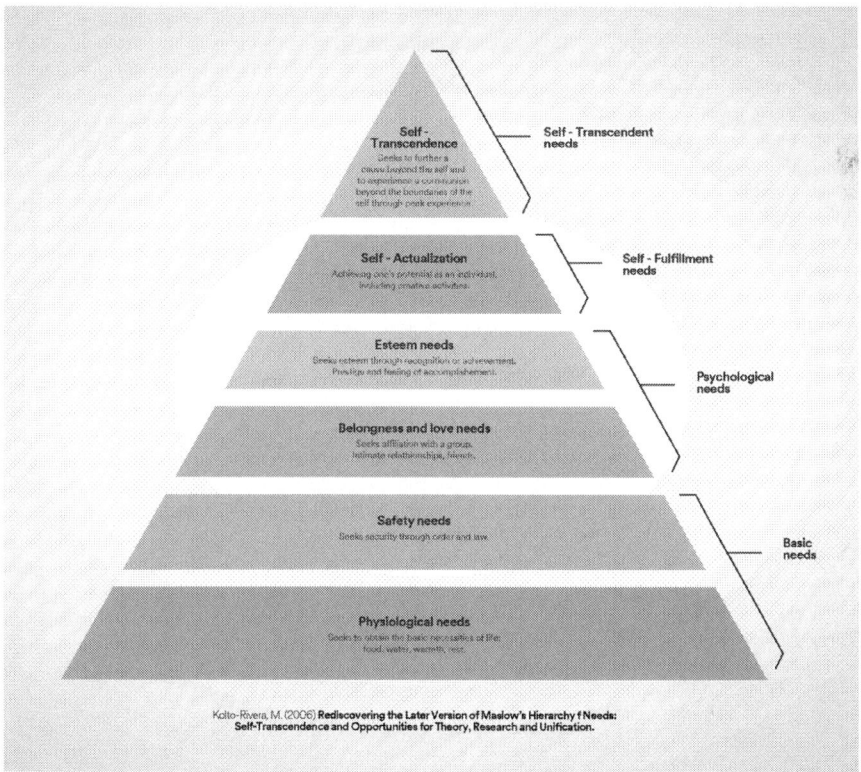

Let's have a look at an updated version of a chart which you've likely seen before: Abraham Maslow's Hierarchy of Human Needs.

One of Maslow's key principles is that the higher (growth) needs *cannot be met until the lower (deficiency) needs have been satisfied.*

Let's consider how things have evolved over the past few thousand years since the agricultural revolution and the birth of modern city- and nation-states.

For the first 99% of this period, Nature was threatening to kill us at every turn. Only 1 out of every 2 people survived until the age of 5. There was no access to clean water, no antibiotics, no waste removal, shelters were constructed by hand and easily destroyed in storms or fires, food had to be hunted or foraged for, and it wasn't certain that the calories spent chasing a deer would pay off.

We were so concerned with our physiological and safety needs – pure survival – that not many of our ancestors had much energy to be concerned with fulfilling our higher level needs for growth. We met our need for love and belonging through our tribe or village, in the joint struggle to survive. Maybe we derived some of our needs for esteem by becoming the Chief or getting a big trophy kill.

Over this period, only small and select groups of privileged humans could have had enough of their needs fulfilled to be able to fully self-actualize. Though there have been exceptions, most of the artists, thinkers, writers, scientists, and philosophers we admire from ancient times were members of the aristocracy or the clergy. In other words, their basic needs were taken care of.

By the year 1800, about 50% of the population in the developed world still worked in agriculture, and mostly for reasons of self-sufficiency.

Today that figure is 2% or less.

In the developed world, we don't think twice about public sewage, garbage collection and disposal, indoor plumbing, and heating systems.

Law enforcement agencies take care of most of our security concerns.

We have social safety nets like social security, pensions, unemployment, disability and health insurances.

We can meet our need for love & belonging (albeit in a low-level way) using social media on our hand-held devices that give us access to billions of conscious souls and the history of human knowledge instantly.

Instead of chasing after your dinner or worrying whether an early frost will kill off the year's crop and starve your family, you can walk to your closest supermarket and have food from all over the world at your fingertips.

We complain about being broke, but forget that thousands of people are at our service in getting that food to us: from the farmers that grew and harvested it, the distributors who washed and packaged it, the shipping services who transported it in refrigerated compartments around the world, the natural gas and oil companies that provided the fuel for transportation, the electricity needed, and the people at your local supermarket who finally sold it to you.

I think I've made my point by now: the deficiency needs for which we have struggled throughout most of recorded history are now fulfilled to the extent that we do not spend much of our conscious thought energy worrying about them.

We are the most privileged generation that humanity has ever known.

In terms of overall quality of life, you are better off than a medieval king. The King – with all his wealth and power – still had to shit in a bucket and wipe his ass with straw.

This begs the question: apart from our financial needs, what role to modern corporations play in meeting our needs?

In his brilliant book *Re-inventing Organizations*, author Frederic Laloux lays out the framework for the history of organizations, and how organizations evolved to meet the most prevalent needs of society at a particular time in history, based on Maslow's hierarchy.

I won't go through his entire framework here – I'll leave it to you to check out Laloux's work, which is amazing and free to download and begin reading immediately – but I will present a short summary of his suppositions about the role of modern corporations, and discuss whether these are still meeting our needs.

Laloux argues that modern companies are mainly organized so as to meet our needs for belonging and esteem. Most corporations talk about a "culture," a set of values that like-minded individuals share. Your work colleagues can go a long way in meeting your need for belonging through the camaraderie of working with others toward a mutually beneficial goal – the success of the company – while sharing a similar set of values, or culture.

Modern corporations also reward success and achievement through promotions, salary increases, performance ratings and bonuses, company cars, and other direct or indirect forms of recognition. This meets our ego-centric needs for esteem and social status.

However, this is as far up the needs pyramid as corporations can typically go. If you are lucky, your corporate job may be helping to meet some of your growth needs – for cognitive growth, maybe even aesthetic growth.

But only in exceedingly rare cases does a corporation allow you to self-actualize through exercising your naturally-given freedom and autonomy to create and reach your full potential.

Let's remember that <u>self-actualization is a need</u>. If you can self-actualize (i.e. your lower needs are fulfilled), then you must self-actualize.

The problem is that it is exceedingly difficult or impossible to self-actualize under a structure of domination, power games, fear and control—unless you learn to inoculate yourself against them.

You are *supposed* to go for the carrot at the end of the stick—and with time, the stick also, so that you can dangle carrots for your own slaves.

But what if you don't like carrots?

A generation with different needs

This is the crux of the problem facing the workplace today.

In one survey of Millennial workers, 87% of respondents said that "professional development and growth" were very important to them in their jobs.

Millennials are simply less willing to wait 3-5 years doing the same thing year after year until the person above them leaves so that they can grow professionally. They would sooner quit and pursue their own growth elsewhere.

This is perceived by the more traditionally-minded as "disloyal," but it's not. It's just that the Millennial might value professional and personal growth over security, and that he or she is prepared to be very loyal to the employer that provided a pathway which allowed them to grow in their own way.

And what about loyalty from the company?

The very notion of "job security" is obsolete. You can be let go at any time for almost any reason.

A decision is taken by some global bigshots thousands of miles away that impacts your line of service, and poof! Your job is gone.

Or you could be let go entirely without justifiable cause – your manager may just not like you.

In fact, just this week I had a phone conversation with a good friend who was fired without cause.

His manager gave him a poor performance rating in spite of having met or exceeded all of the goals they had mutually agreed upon. When my friend challenged the performance rating, the manager had IT investigate his computer usage time. They discovered that he was not active at his computer for the entire 8.2 hours each day as contractually required. As if *anyone* sat at their desks for that amount of time during the workday without collaborating with colleagues or attending meetings.

The conclusion of IT was enough to hold up the manager's decision, and now my friend, the sole earner supporting a family of four, finds himself suddenly unemployed on a manager's whim after more than 10 years of service to the company.

At a previous job, the decision was made to let one of my colleagues go due to budget cuts. My manager was informed, but was forbidden to say anything to this person. For months, she was instructed to sit on the information until the latest possible moment, when top management "allowed" her to communicate the layoff.

Not only are you controlled and dis-empowered, but you don't even have the job security that is supposed to come with sacrificing your freedom.

This is the most empowered human generation that has ever been born. We have grown up with the Internet. We are used to the free decentralization of information. We do not understand why our bosses do not allow more flexibility in the workplace when almost anything can be done online now. The idea that you can't work from home – or anywhere else – just does not click for us anymore.

I have had this argument with management many times. Sometimes (I always like to push against the rules) I would not show up to the office for work, as I had no meetings scheduled and had decided to work remotely.

Usually I got a reprimanding from management, their reason being that "they didn't know where I was" and that people "were looking for me but since I was not at my desk one of my colleagues had to cover the work".

I told them that it was crap. I had a company mobile phone, was online over the intra-office messenger all day, and someone could have simply messaged, called, or e-mailed me.

They will argue that it is about being productive, team solidarity or something else, but there is never a good reason. It is only about power and control.

This is the conflict of ideas which occurs when most of leadership consists of the "old guard" who have a very different idea from Millennials when it comes to work, and the needs that should be fulfilled through work.

I. Where You Are Now

To express things more visually, this is another chart you've likely seen before demonstrating the exponential growth of human technological progress:

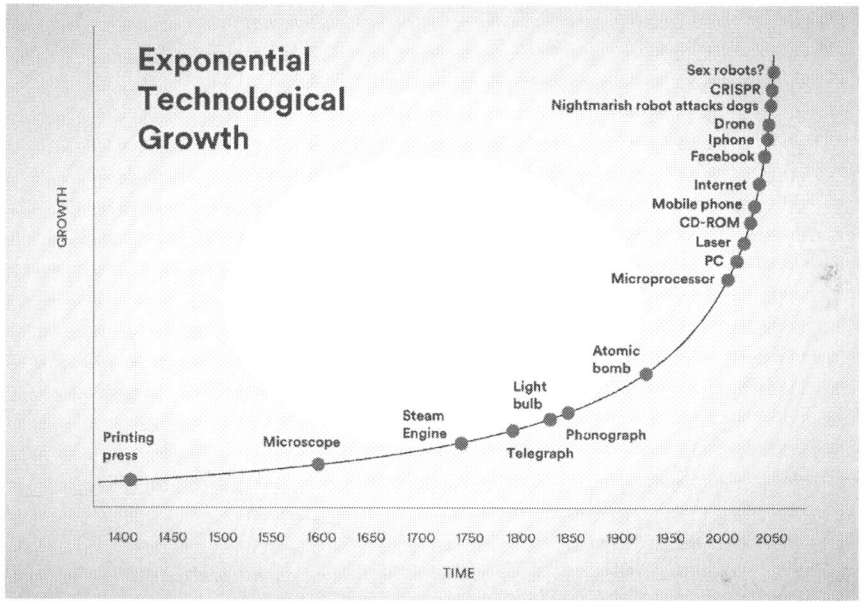

The evolution of our needs has followed a similar trend line.

As technology has exponentially increased and made the fulfillment of our basic needs exponentially easier, the newest generation is able to think more about their higher level needs of growth, self-actualization, and transcendence.

Most corporations just have not kept pace with this trend. We are evolving at a faster pace than at any other point in human history. Company leadership is often in their 50s and 60s, yet this age gap of 20-30 years might as well be an unbridgeable chasm. Leadership simply does not understand the needs of the new generation because they grew up and progressed in their careers in a different context, and work fulfilled their needs in a different way.

Therefore it should not come as a surprise that Millenials are quitting their jobs to pursue entrepreneurship, become yoga teachers, health and life coaches, and travel the world as digital nomads in ever increasing numbers. The old command and control, "show up at the office from 9 to 5" patriarchal models just don't work for us anymore.

We are tired of being treated like children.

If we can make decisions in our private lives, we can also make them in our professional ones.

Autonomy is a need and a natural right. It is not something to be earned or which requires permission.

The first companies to truly understand and embrace this fact will get all of the top young talent.

—

There is some hope. In his book, Frederic Laloux introduces the concept of a holacracy.

A holacracy is the newest form of organization that is shaping around the evolution of our highest needs. It is a truly decentralized model of working.

In a holacracy, authority and decision-making are distributed across self-organizing teams, rather than being concentrated in a typical management hierarchy. It is a much more empowering company model and the research around them has been extremely promising and interesting.

A holacracy is probably the most advanced structural model in the slowly emerging trend of creating democratic businesses. Slowly, leaders are beginning to realize that the newest generation is not going to accept the old ways of working, and that new models of decision-making will be needed if they are to attract the best talent and remain competitive. These models are more empowering and allow business to react with much greater agility.

However, in order for a typical organization to adopt a holacracy as its working model, it must first completely destroy its existing structure. That means saying goodbye to HR departments, Finance, Operations and Sales divisions, and restructuring everything into smaller, self-governing teams.

Turning an existing company into a holacracy would require a level of honesty, daring and trust amongst leadership that I have yet to see in my experience. A great number of department leaders will push against it as they attempt to justify their existence.

But with any change, it will happen once a critical mass is reached. When enough people decide that the status quo is unacceptable, then massive change will come.

Your Primary Human Needs

Unless you're one of the lucky ones reading this and thinking, "Now I know why I love my job so much!" you've probably come to the realization that your corporate job may not be the best place for you to self-actualize.

Great, you've shown me the problem – now what? I still have no idea what I should do!

The first step in gaining more clarity about the kind of life you want to live is to begin cultivating greater self-awareness.

> Socrates: *"To know thyself is the beginning of wisdom".*

Identifying your primary driving human needs is a useful starting place for discovering what you need in order to feel happy, successful, and fulfilled in life.

There are a number of different models categorizing human needs. Anthony Robbins created a powerful and simple model of 6 human needs. Marshall Rosenberg put them into 7 categories, whereas Chilean economist Manfred Max-Neef proposed 9 primary needs.

After studying the various models I have come to believe that there are 7 main categories of human needs.

You will notice that this model closely parallels that of Maslow, just applied in a different way.

The 7 Human Needs

SECURITY
VARIETY
FEELING OF IMPORTANCE
CONNECTION/LOVE
GROWTH
SERVICE
AUTONOMY

It is better to think of these needs as categories, rather than limiting their interpretation to only certain words.

For you, **Security** could mean a feeling of certainty, comfort, stability, predictability, safety, or structure.

Variety could mean exhilaration, uncertainty, unpredictability, spontaneity, or taking risks.

Feeling of Importance may refer to respect, achievement, recognition, gaining approval, or feeling significant.

Connection can be romantic love, friendship, being neighborly, familial love, or feeling you are part of a community of like minds, that you belong somewhere.

Growth typically refers to learning, evolving, acquiring new skills, developing, and getting out of your comfort zone.

Service is your need to give back to others. It could be volunteering, donating to charity, teaching, sharing your skills, or contributing to your community or fellow humans in other ways.

And **Autonomy** can also mean feeling independent, responsible, making your own choices, feeling free to express yourself creatively, and being held accountable for your actions.

———

Everyone – from the lowly employee to the CEO of your company – has the same fundamental needs. Depending on who you are and what your life experiences have been, you will emphasize some needs over others.

I once had a German work colleague who fits every stereotype you probably have about Germans. Prior to joining the company he had spent 8 years working for the *Bundeswehr* – the German military – and had a very strong need for predictability and structure.

He arrived at 06:50 each morning and left at 15:50 every afternoon. He ate the same sandwich at his desk for lunch at 12:00. He would only ever go out for lunch with the team if we had planned it in advance. He had his daily 09:00

snack, a particular kind of cookie. When discussing a specific work topic – even if it was a short discussion – he would put an invitation in the calendar and when the time came, he would swivel around in his chair toward me (he sat right next to me) and open the topic.

When I met him, he had been in the same role for 7 years in a company with very high annual turnover. In fact, he had been there longer than nearly everyone else working in our department.

He found a structure that worked for him and he stuck to it.

In contrast, my need for Security is much lower and is expressed differently. I get bored doing the same type of work in the same environment for too long. I have never worked the same job for more than 3 years. Somehow I always knew this about myself; I even began worrying that I had some form of ADD.

When I understood myself in terms of the 7 Human Needs, it immediately became clear to me why I felt so bored when my boss laid out my career plans the way he did. Like my German colleague, my boss also had a relatively high need for stability and structure. Perhaps my German colleague would have felt overjoyed had he been presented with the same future.

My needs for Variety and Growth simply outweigh my need for Security.

Just because I have a low need for security doesn't mean that it isn't a need. I just meet the need in other ways. For instance, I have roughly the same routine each morning, I eat basically the same breakfast every day, and when I am feeling low or tired, I comfort myself by watching Seinfeld reruns or Netflix. I like to keep a certain amount of cash in my bank account, which makes me feel secure knowing that I have a bit of a safety net. Others may require more, and still others might feel fine walking around without any money or possessions at all.

The point is that each person is unique, has an emphasis on certain needs over others, and meets them in different ways.

Needs Exercise #1:

For this exercise, refer to the below template. If you are reading this on paperback you can write in it directly (don't worry if you mess it up, I will include all exercise sheets in the Appendix so you can print it out if needed). Or re-produce it on a sheet of paper if you prefer.

Need	Ranking	When do I feel that this need is met?
Security		(ex: Having a regular income)
Variety		(ex: trying a new hobby)
Feeling of Importance		(ex: my boss praises me for good work on a project)
Connection		
Growth		
Service		
Autonomy		

Step 1: Rank each need in order of importance to you. Do not think about it too much – go with your gut.

Step 2: For each need, ask yourself the question: "What needs to happen in order for me to feel that this need is met?" Write down as many answers as you can and take as long as you like. For example:

→ What do you need to feel like you have security in your life? Is it job security? A certain amount in your bank account? Being around familiar people? Knowing that someone will be there when you come home?

→ What gives you variety? Meeting new friends? Joining new clubs? Trying out new hobbies? Watching different kinds of movies?

→ What makes you feel important? Receiving praise or recognition from certain people or in front of certain people? Your job title or salary? A nice photo of you on Instagram that gets a lot of "likes", hearts, and comments?

→ How do you feel connected to others? If you are in a relationship, what specific things do you need from your partner to feel loved? If you are dating, what makes you feel that spark? How do you define "friendship", or an act of friendship? When do you know that you are "clicking" with someone? What do you want out of a community?

→ When do you feel you are growing? What are you learning? When do you feel like you are stretching the boundary of your comfort zone? When do you feel you are improving or evolving as a person?

→ How do you like to serve others? What does "contribution" mean for you? In which ways do you feel you are contributing to the betterment or happiness of others? Is there a specific cause or charity that you believe in?

→ Do you feel autonomous and independent in your work and personal relationships? Does your work allow you enough freedom to create and execute your own processes? Does it give you the space to feel creative? Are you encouraged to take charge and responsibility for your actions?

Step 3: For the next several days to a week, observe your behavior in daily life and reflect on your activities and behavior in light of your answers in the template.

Step 4: Re-visit the ranking and adjust if needed.

I. Where You Are Now

Your needs are not a constant

You may discover that the needs you thought were most important to you are not finding expression, or that you are more concerned with some needs than you originally thought.

Your needs will change over time depending on who you are, where you come from, and where you are in life. Your need for security will be higher if you have a child or loved one to take care of, than if you are young, single and unattached. It could be different from month to month, or week to week.

The 7 Human Needs also have a certain flow hierarchy, like in Maslow's model:

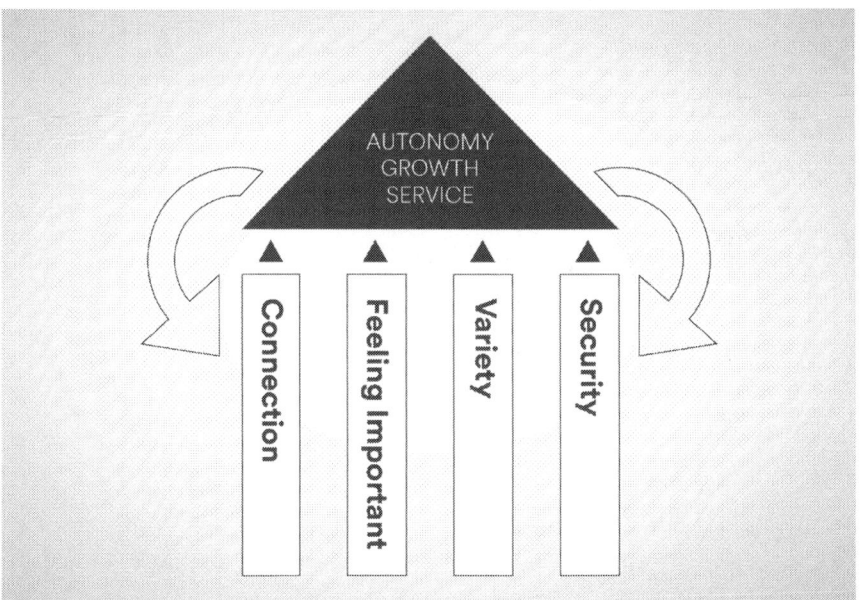

Growth, Service, and Autonomy can be considered the "higher" needs. These are the needs dealing mainly with self-expression and transcendence.

Unless your 4 "lower" needs are already fulfilled to varying degrees, you may not be able to focus on meeting your "higher" level needs.

If you don't have a solid and secure foundation, you cannot build a superstructure reaching the sky.

If you don't have love or connection – whether it be from friends, family, yourself, or God – who will root for your success? Who will pick you up when you stumble?

If you don't feel respected, admired, or appreciated, it will be difficult to acquire the confidence needed to pursue your biggest dreams.

If you feel that your life is boring, monotonous, and devoid of variety, you may not have the stimulation necessary to spark your creativity.

Likewise, you may have noticed that you can fulfill some of your lower level needs *through* the higher level ones.

For instance, contributing to others by organizing a fundraiser to help people in need may also help you meet your need for connection and significance, when someone gives you a hug and recognizes you for your efforts.

Meeting your need for growth can simultaneously meet your need for variety, for example by taking a course on a new subject.

And exercising autonomy may also give you a feeling of importance and security, by making you feel powerful and in control.

Needs Exercise #2:

It is important to make the point that our needs can be met in ways that are beneficial or detrimental to ourselves and to others. A *destructive* habit can also meet certain needs.

As Anthony Robbins has remarked: "any habit that meets 3 or more needs becomes an addiction."

For instance, overeating typically fulfills the need for Security/Comfort and for connecting to yourself. Eating a variety of fattening and tasty junk food may serve as a "reward" to yourself for certain behaviors, like binge eating cake and chocolate when you feel sad.

The need for Connection is often met in self-destructive ways. For example, becoming addicted to "likes" on social media while not taking the time to be present and be with people in "meatspace". Or being overly dramatic, indulging in self-pity, seeking the pity of others, or engaging in emotional "hostage taking" (i.e. "I will only show you love if you do X, Y, or Z").

I. Where You Are Now

Smoking cigarettes can fulfill a need for variety (it gives you something to do when you feel bored), comfort (rewarding yourself), connection (socializing with other smokers), and even significance (feeling "cool").

Even Growth can have negative consequences if it comes at the expense of others' well-being.

Take a moment now to review your list. Try and identify both positive and negative ways you may be meeting each need.

NEED	HOW DO I MEET THIS NEED? (Positive)	HOW DO I MEET THIS NEED? (Negative)
Security		
Variety		
Feeling Important		
Connection		
Growth		
Service		
Autonomy		

Applying the 7 human needs to specific life zones

The 7 Human Needs model can be applied to your life as a whole, and you can also use this model as a lens to examine specific aspects of your life.

Until now we have mostly been discussing work, so go through each of the needs again, asking yourself, "How does my job meet my needs"?

If you work at a good company and have a competent boss, your career probably helps you in part to meet your needs for certainty, connection and significance. You know where you go each day and feel like you have some security, you enjoy connecting and sharing ideas with your colleagues and you are rewarded and recognized for good work through either tangible or intangible rewards.

You may feel like you are contributing if your role allows you to use your knowledge to solve problems. It may give you lots of variety via diverse projects. It may even help you meet your need for growth if your career assists you in learning new things and taking you out of your comfort zone. You may feel a degree of autonomy over how you arrange your work day, and how you execute your tasks.

The 7 Human Needs model can also be applied to other areas of your life.

For instance, you can examine any relationship – romantic, platonic, or familial – by asking yourself needs-based questions:

- → Do I feel certain in my relationship? Is it based on trust?

- → Do we experience variety together? How?

- → Am I making time to connect? Are we present with each other and how? Are we communicating from a place of total honesty and trust?

- → Does he/she make me feel important to him/her, special, and appreciated?

- → Is my relationship growing? Does it allow me to grow in my own way? Are we growing together?

- → Have we both committed to contributing to the relationship? How do I contribute? What is my role?

→ Do I feel a sense of independence within the relationship? Does he or she give me the space to grow in my own way? What would they say if you told them that you couldn't see them for a while because you needed to do something important for your own self-development?

You can do the same thing with any of your life zones, from your friends and community to your spiritual life.

Human Needs Exercise #3: Life Zones

Step 1: Divide your life into at least 3 life zones. There are no rules here, you can split it up any way you like. One useful way to do this is to draw a circle, and create a pie chart. Each "slice" of the chart is the proportion of time you spend thinking about this area of your life on an average day.

For example: My Family, My Career, My Relationships, My Community, My Well-Being, My Spiritual Life, etc.

Step 2: For each life zone, go through the needs and identify how your needs are met in that particular life zone. You can use the chart below, I have filled in some examples.

NEED	LIFE ZONE		
	My Career	My Relationships	My Passion/Hobby
Security	Steady paycheck, place to go everyday, routine	I know my loved ones will be there for me	I know I can do this, and when I practice I will enjoy it
Variety			
Feeling Important			
Connection			
Growth			
Service			
Autonomy			

II.
Quit Your Bitching

This next step is extremely important.

Right now, you need to acknowledge that you are exactly where you are based on the decisions you have made.

This may be a difficult thing to accept.

Until now you have probably felt a victim, a passive participant, rocked by the waves of the uncontrollable forces of life.

Your current position in life was due to circumstances outside of your control – your upbringing, the government, unlucky situations, unfortunate events, evil corporations, whatever.

To some extent this is true.

It is true that everyone has a different set of starting circumstances – socioeconomic situation, DNA, family, constitution, and metabolism – there is an endless variety of "starting factors" that influence your trajectory and the ease or difficulty of particular areas of your life.

Some people begin the game of life as invincible Super Star Man Mario, and others the little Mario that can be smashed by one touch of a harmless Goomba.

It is also true that things in life "just happen" at random, and bad things can and will happen to all of us, seemingly without reason or meaning.

However, it is your <u>reaction</u> to the situation that determines everything. Your reaction, and your subsequent decision is a choice that you make, and this is entirely within your control.

Nearly everything in life is a choice, and you are imprisoning yourself mainly with the language you use.

You may be thinking to yourself:

> *"What do you mean everything is a choice? I HAVE to go to work. I HAVE to pay my bills. I HAVE to pay back my student loans. I HAVE to pay for my kids' schooling."*

No – you actually don't **HAVE** to do any of those things.

You have chosen to pay your bills because you like to have the comfort of electricity, heat, running water and plumbing, and Netflix in your home.

You like being in contact with others and accessing the Internet at any time so you've purchased a mobile phone plan.

You don't want to be a homeless bum that begs family and friends for money so you've taken an apartment or house and pay your bills.

You value keeping your commitments so you have chosen to pay off your debts.

You decided to have children and you want them to have a traditional education so you've decided to send them to school.

There are examples of people who have chosen NOT to do these things:

- → There are people who choose not to communicate over the phone and don't have mobile Internet or use social media
- → There are people who live in bungalows on the beach without electricity
- → There are people who roam the earth with nothing but the clothes on their back and their meager possessions in a wheeled cart
- → There are people who have defaulted on their debts and declared bankruptcy
- → There are people who homeschool their kids
- → There are people who grow their own food or help on organic farms in exchange for food and accommodation

I'm not making this up. I have personally met people in each category from the above list, and I bet you've at least heard about someone – a friend of a friend, that guy from university – who has done something similar.

There was a story about a German guy who spent more than 4 years [living practically without money](1) – and he has a young daughter!

Once you understand the underlying reasons behind your choices, you may feel a sense of relief, even pride.

Whenever you find yourself trapped, change the language you use when thinking about that situation.

You show up to work on time every day not because you have to, but because you want to do a good job and keep it.

You want to keep your job because of the comfort and sense of security it gives you, and the financial reward which allows you to purchase things you enjoy and to fulfill your financial commitments.

You want a roof over your head, a certain level of comfort in your home, to experience the joy of being a parent, and a structured educational environment for your children.

You do want that vintage wine collection, the expensive ski holidays in the Swiss Alps, that new car.

Or maybe you just realized that you don't really need or want any of these things, because your desire to be autonomous, flexible, and value of time over money is greater than the prestige, significance or feeling of satisfaction you get from these things.

The only real question here is the level of comfort that you want, the kind of life you want, and what you need and value.

You could highly value your free time, have no desire to own a home or accumulate material possessions, and feel no sense of obligation to your financial commitments. If so, then you are doing the wrong thing by staying in your job to pay back your debts, and you should quit your job, declare bankruptcy, downsize your home and live out of a van down by the river.

There is no right or wrong answer here, as everyone has a different set of values and I am not here to pass judgment on what you "should" do.

---

1   https://www.huffingtonpost.com/2013/02/28/raphael-fellmer-no-money_n_2782543.html

You may also have begun to realize that some of your decisions were not made consciously, but rather have been unconsciously dictated by the expectations or norms of family or society.

That's okay. It happens to all of us. You can acknowledge this.

But now you're becoming more awake and aware. You can consciously decide what happens going forward, and choose how you feel about the decisions you've already made.

Remember though, that you don't *HAVE* to do anything. All you need to do is survive – and even that is a choice.

The possible modes of living and being are as numerous and varied as there are people in this world.

You just need to ask yourself *WHY* you are doing the things you do, and to remind yourself of this from time to time.

Whenever you become frustrated about your job, remind yourself of the underlying reasons for being in the job.

How is this job helping you to get where you need to go? What needs is it fulfilling?

If you are just doing it for the money, what are you going to do with the money?

Are you using it towards something that will bring you longer term satisfaction, freedom, or growth?

Or does your pay check vanish each month on hookers and blow?

Depending on your answer, you are either on a pathway to freedom, or you're serving a life sentence in a virtual prison.

YOU

II. Quit Your Bitching

ARE

II. Quit Your Bitching

GOING

II. Quit Your Bitching

TO

DIE.

II. Quit Your Bitching

> *"We have two lives, and the second begins when we realize that we only have one."*
> Confucius

Take a moment to acknowledge this.

Let it settle in your mind.

I am not trying to play on your natural fear of death – I am simply trying to draw your awareness to the truth of your mortality.

Our fear of death unites us all. It makes us brothers and sisters. But even though we all share this fear, we rarely talk about or acknowledge it.

In our minds, our death is typically someday far off into the distant future, when we're old, retired, and ready to rest after a life well lived.

In our daily lives, we act as though it's never going to happen, and we make plans as if we know *when* it will happen.

Many of us are stuck in situations or routines and not feeling good about them.

We think, *someday, when I retire...*

If I won the lottery, then...

If I didn't have to do X anymore, then...

Then... only then!

Then, you will *finally* find happiness and freedom, because then you will finally have the time and means to do that Thing You've Always Wanted to Do.

It's never now. You never act on it now. You delay, certain that you will be able to do it later.

But what if there is no later?

You've probably heard it so often that it has become a cliché.

Eastern wisdom traditions have been teaching it for thousands of years.

There is only today. There is only the Now. If tomorrow decides to come for you, it is a blessing.

II. Quit Your Bitching

I have been blessed with a strange kind of fortune – a fortune that is impossible to obtain through work or any physical means.

At the time of writing this book, the relatively young age of 35, I had already had 4 extremely personal encounters with Death.

When I was 18, I went for a swim in Newport, Rhode Island.

It was a hot summer day. We were walking along a small local road. Next to the road was an inlet from the Atlantic Ocean. The water looked clear, cool and refreshing.

I jumped in.

And was sucked instantly into an underwater tunnel.

Fully submerged under water, I struggled against the shockingly powerful current to try to reach the edge of the cement tunnel.

My panicked mind raced: *if I can just grab onto the edge, I can pull myself out.*

I was a strong swimmer, but it was no use. The current was unbelievably strong. My hands were just a few centimeters from the edge, clawing, scraping against the sides of the tunnel.

I couldn't make any progress. The edge was *so* close. Despite all my effort I was slowly slipping further into the tunnel.

I risked a look over my shoulder behind me.

Only darkness. A black tunnel full of water. Certain death.

I could see no exit, no sliver of light indicating an escape.

It's true what they say in these moments. My life began to flash before my eyes. I saw newspaper headlines:

Idiot kid dies by drowning in Newport, Rhode Island. What a waste of a life.

Maybe a minute or two went by. My breath was running out.

With no other option, I surrendered. I gave up the struggle and let the water take me deeper into the tunnel.

To my extreme good fortune, there was a pocket of air at the top of the tunnel. I thanked the Universe or God or whatever might be there for the air, for a few more moments of life.

The water then drew me out the other side of the tunnel, which was on the opposite side of the small road. The tunnel had connected the Atlantic inlet with a pond on the other side of the road.

I crawled out of the water, in shock and full of adrenaline.

I was alive!

My fingers were ruined. Slashed and bloody from scraping at the cement tunnel. Cut so deep that I am still missing fingerprints on two of my fingers.

Fuck my fingers. I was alive!

—

One year later.

I was 19 and probably in the best shape of my life.

I was in the gym, the swimming pool, or both every day of the week. I was also playing competitive racquetball for my university a further 3-5 times a week.

One Friday morning, I was sitting at home eating cereal. It was about 10.30 AM. I was taking summer classes but didn't have any class that day, so was planning to go to the gym.

Suddenly I began to feel a crushing sensation around my chest and abdomen.

At first I thought it was a strange kind of indigestion. So I lie down for 20 minutes.

The crushing feeling began to localize around my chest. My left arm went numb. Then my right arm. It felt like a giant constrictor snake had wrapped itself around my chest, squeezing the air out of my lungs. Breathing became difficult.

I thought, *this can't be happening. Am I having a heart attack?*

I didn't dare call an ambulance. What if I was wrong? I would look like an idiot.

So I drove myself to the hospital.

Stupid idea.

Luckily it was a short 10 minute drive and I remained conscious.

I walked up to the registration desk and spoke with the nurse there.

"Excuse me... I know this sounds crazy... but I think I'm having a heart attack."

"I see. Do you have any final exams coming up?" the nurse asked. It was the week before summer finals.

"Yes, I do," I told her.

"Are you stressed about them?"

"No, not really."

She directed me to go and speak with another nurse.

This nurse asked me to sit down, and then rate my pain on a scale from 1 to 10.

"A 1 indicates no pain, and 10 is the worst pain you can imagine".

I tried to imagine the worst pain imaginable. I thought of torture devices from the Spanish Inquisition. Being drawn and quartered, and burned alive.

That would be a 10.

Compared to that, then my pain was probably a 4 or a 5.

I told her 4.

I was then instructed to sit in a waiting area, and that another nurse would come by shortly to pick me up.

So I sat and waited.

And waited.

20 minutes went by...

Then 30 minutes.

40 minutes passed and I was doubled over in pain, worse than ever, and slowly losing consciousness. My vision was becoming blurry and the edges of my peripheral vision had begun to fade.

I mustered up some strength and staggered back to reception.

"Listen... I know you think I'm some stupid kid worried about his exams, but I think something is seriously wrong here," I pleaded.

"Oh, there you are!" she said. "The nurse was looking for you. Here she comes".

Another nurse then immediately guided me to a bed in the general ward.

I was given some anti-anxiety medication while the doctors took my blood. After a few minutes they took me to do an electrocardiogram.

Then I lie on the bed and waited some more. The pain was as bad as ever.

II. Quit Your Bitching

At some point a doctor gave me something else. Nitroglycerin. I put it under my tongue. It tasted coppery, like putting your tongue on the electrodes of a battery.

The chest pain was gone in 5 minutes.

Then another doctor came by with some questions.

"Did you smoke crack?"

I told him I didn't.

He walked away, brows furrowed, muttering to himself.

Another doctor. "We think you had a heart attack."

No shit, I told him.

After they had established that I did indeed have a heart attack in spite of being a fit, extremely active and healthy 19 year old, they ran some tests.

I was in the hospital for a weekend. They monitored me. Everything was fine.

They performed a procedure which involved putting a radioactive dye into my blood to check for arterial blockages.

0% blockage. Clean as a whistle.

While I was in the hospital, teams of residents would come by to talk to me. I was something of a research specimen.

Most of them seemed mystified.

The final diagnosis?

Vasospasm.

A clinical term which means that an artery can spasm and close off at random, shutting off blood flow to the heart.

Though the probability is extremely low, like an aneurysm, anyone could have it.

———

April 2011.

I was staying with my mom in a hotel in Phnom Penh, Cambodia.

A month earlier I had been diagnosed with an extremely rare type of migraine called *hemiplegic migraine.* It seemed to be related to whatever quality of my blood that had triggered my heart attack years before.

II. Quit Your Bitching

The headaches began occurring suddenly and without any obvious trigger.

They are one of the most aggressive and dangerous types of migraine. In addition to the headache that renders any type of normal daily functioning impossible, the symptoms also include vomiting, partial to total paralysis, loss of speech, and complete confusion up to total loss of consciousness.

It is difficult to express the frustration of having a complete thought in your head but being totally unable to express it. And the confusion. If you can equate your normal field of conscious experience to looking through a large lens, it is like experiencing the world through a lens which has been cracked into 100 pieces.

The headaches and symptoms can last up to 72 hours.

We were only in Phnom Penh for a few days when a migraine struck. It was the worst one I had ever had.

After 12 hours of vomiting, paralysis and loss of speech, my mom – being a nurse – realized the gravity of the situation and put me into the one and only international clinic that Phnom Penh had. I couldn't keep anything down, not even water.

She phoned a friend in the medical profession who overnight posted some emergency medication.

I had been running an extremely high fever and my brain had begun to swell.

I was so dehydrated that my piss had turned into Coca-Cola.

Without that medication, my brain would have continued to swell and I likely would have had a stroke, or worse.

—

Taiwan, November 2009.

It was late afternoon and I was having passionate sex with my then-fiancée. My phone rang and I let it go to voicemail.

After we finished I listened to the message.

It was my mom. She asked me to call her back.

Now? It must have been 4 a.m. in New York.

Dread.

II. Quit Your Bitching

I called her back.

She was in tears.

"Dad's dead," was all she managed to say.

He was 59 years old.

There was nothing wrong with him. He was very active and healthy.

It was an accident. He had been setting up a high tree stand for deer hunting. Something went wrong with the mechanism and it launched him over 10 meters down onto the forest floor below.

Just like that – gone. He was already long dead when they found his body.

This is the kind of stuff that you hear about in the news. A car crash, a bus accident, a shooting.

But it always happens to other people – never to you.

Though writing these stories is certainly cathartic for me, that is not my main reason for doing it.

We unfortunately are not appreciative of the ephemeral nature of life until something terrible impacts us directly. We get into an accident and narrowly escape death, or we receive some awful diagnosis.

Only then do we really reflect on our mortality and ask ourselves difficult questions.

What am I doing with my life?

What is most important to me?

What would I die for?

How can I make best use of the limited time on this earth?

If I died tomorrow, would I feel like I had done everything I needed to do?

When can I feel that I've had a life that was well-lived?

You've probably heard this type of story before. A woman, miserable, is diagnosed with cancer and has 6 months to live. She then decides to live the last 6 months to the fullest – visits Macchu Picchu, goes skydiving, climbs Kilimanjaro, runs with the bulls.

Miraculously, her cancer goes into remission.

I don't know if it's possible to really gain a deep appreciation of the fragility of life, and the mission to really start putting your dreams into action NOW, without a direct experience that enables you to consider the simple fact that tomorrow may never come.

Even having had such experiences myself, we are quick to forget. A few months go by and we are back on autopilot, thinking we'll live forever again.

It's something we need to be reminded of. Not to the level of neurotic worry, but just to the level of awareness.

I am hoping that my stories are sufficiently vivid and of a random enough nature that you could imagine them happening to you or someone in your family.

What would you do differently today, if you knew that tomorrow would never come?

How would you change your communication with others?

What would you drop?

What would you start doing right now?

We all have the same basic fears.

That's why the use of fear as a control mechanism is so effective: fears are universal.

The only way to inoculate yourself against fear is to acknowledge and understand it.

There are really only 2 primary fears from which all lesser fears are derived:

- → Fear of Loss of Love
- → Fear of Death

Thus, when you are stressed at work or afraid of your boss, you are afraid primarily for 2 reasons:

- → that you will be criticized or shamed in front of others, and will lose their respect (Fear of Loss of Love);
- → that you will be fired, and will subsequently lose the respect of colleagues, friends, and family (Fear of Loss of Love), and you will never find another job, have no money, wind up homeless and starve (Fear of Death)

That's why the fear of being fired is so great. It hits both your primal fears in one blow.

The next time you worry, or are afraid of someone or something, remember that it always fits into one of these 2 categories.

Then think about them each in turn and ask yourself if your fear is based in truth.

If you worry about your job for example, is it really the case that you will die if you get fired?

Probably not, right? You will be able to find another job or some other way to make money. In the developed world, there are usually safety nets like unemployment and social assistance. You probably have family and friends who will help you get back on your feet.

When your boss criticizes you in front of others, will you lose the love of your closest ones? The people you *REALLY* care about?

True love is unconditional. You might temporarily lose someone's respect, sure, but then you should ask yourself why you crave this person's respect in the first place, and why they have so much power over you. What relationship could it be a proxy for?

We spend a lot of time worrying about the opinions of people that we don't really care about.

And if you have sufficient Self-Love, it can never be taken away.

The next time you are afraid of someone, remember that they are afraid of the same things in different ways.

In this way you are the same. You share the same experience of being human, no matter what their title or how much money they make.

II. Quit Your Bitching

You both crave the love and respect of others, and are afraid of it being taken away.

And in the end… you will both exit life the same way. Afraid and stripped of everything that might have mattered to you.

There is no "destroying" fear. You can silence it for a time, but it will always creep back.

All you can do is bring your awareness to it and work on it.

You must ask for the things you want

Here's the thing: if you've begun to hate your job, or it just bores you and you feel as though your current career trajectory offers no room for growth, no one is going to hold your hand, raise you up to the next level and find a new challenge for you.

You are performing and leadership is happy with the *status quo*: thriving off of your precious time that you have exchanged to them for a specific number in your bank account each month.

A good boss will make you feel like you can have an honest and trusting dialogue with him/her about your career aspirations, without making you fearful of being fired simply for stating your desires for a change in assignment, more money, or more responsibility.

If you work for an exceptional organization, your boss and the leadership will do whatever they can to make connections within the company and try to help you build out that career path for you. They generally want to keep people who want to be there.

But you must do a good job. And you must **ask**.

It's amazing to me the number of people I have coached who desire a thing but won't ask for it.

And when I say ask...really it's a form of demand. You must "ask" from a place of power and strength.

While I was working at the huge international consultancy, almost all of my colleagues would talk about how they would love to go on a short term international assignment. They would talk about someone who got this great assignment and complain about how it wasn't fair.

Can you guess how many of them actually asked for an assignment?

Zero.

Asking for something you want is a simple thing that seems to be loaded with fear.

II. Quit Your Bitching

Once you fixate on a particular wish for your future, the familiar thoughts come: "But who am I to ask? Why do I deserve that? What if they say no? I am really fine where I am, I don't need to rock the boat".

Your mind will tell you all kinds of stories, in order to avoid that dreaded outcome: Rejection. You will talk yourself out of action.

Your mind is the most powerful tool you have at your disposal. But it can also be your toughest opponent. It wants to protect you. It sees what you have been doing and knows that your human organism has been successfully surviving under your current conditions.

In your mind's interpretation, any change comes with the potential risk that you will not survive the new future, so it will fight you through change until you re-program it into obedience.

We hate it when people say "no" to us. When someone says "no" to our idea or suggestion, we take it as a rejection of our entire selves. We feel ashamed to ask. It is painful. And just as we seek pleasure, we avoid pain.

It's a manifestation of the slave mentality. We have been conditioned to accept whatever our dear leaders have given us ("The economy is bad and you are lucky enough to have a job"), to be grateful that we even have a job.

There are people starving in India. I have a good job, a roof over my head, food on the table. Who am I to ask for more?

Now you definitely should be grateful for what you have, and you should make it a daily practice to spend time in gratitude and appreciation.

But you should _also_ ask for more.

What if you had more money to actually help those starving people in India?

The more you ask for, the more you have, and the more utility is in your control to express yourself and have an impact on the world, should you so desire.

Asking is the way you project your desires out into the Universe.

Take the asking as a feedback mechanism. You want Something, so you ask for it. If you are told No, it just means that you might not get that Something from your current circumstances. So either the circumstances need to change, or you need to change the way you ask. This is valuable feedback.

Rejection isn't a nice feeling, but ironically the only way to overcome it is to be rejected more often. So you need to ask more often.

When asking for something, you should always remain optimistic. If you're doing well and people respect you at work, they will try to keep you. But even the greatest boss might not be happy if you say that you want to change roles – especially if you are a good performer and have earned a lot of revenue for your business.

Your boss is likely to feel out the power of your intention. He wants to know how solid your position is, and to what extent you will stay in your role if he tells you No.

If things go well and you get a Yes, then you need to press for specifics. Your boss might say something like, "I will look into it". Ask for a definite *when* they will look into it and *when* you can expect an answer. Say that you want to take up this topic again in a few weeks.

Be persistent.

Again, even the best leadership is probably happy to keep things the way they are. It is less work for them, and it is costly to replace you.

Expect a Yes, but be prepared for a No.

Make a logical case, rehearse your arguments, anticipate how you will respond when your boss gives objections, and weigh your options in case of a No.

How strong is your desire for the Something?

What will you do if your boss says No?

Is it a deal breaker for you? Or will you remain in your job?

It's your choice; it's within your power and control.

It has often been the case for me that when I asked for something – like the chance to work at home one day a week, or to work part time – I was told No.

Depending on what you ask for, it is very likely that you will also be told No at first.

Leadership will assume that your fear is strong enough to keep you in your job. Or that your request will create a lot of similar requests from your colleagues and that it would rock the boat too much.

Remember, they need to keep everyone "in line".

They interpret your desire as a simple request, and they will assume that – like them – you also would rather maintain the *status quo*; and that the effort of finding a new job, or the uncertainty of quitting your job is too great in comparison to the request you've made.

So you need to decide how important the Thing is to you, and what you demand for yourself and your life.

I have observed that most people who eventually got what they wanted were fully prepared to walk away. They were told No at first, and they valued the Thing so strongly that they informed management that they were going to begin their job search; after which, the answer suddenly became a Yes.

The same thing happened to me.

I had a long commute and asked to work from home one day per week. I was told something about there being "a home office Policy" and that "they needed to check with top management". My boss didn't give me a clear answer and eventually I was told that the Policy only applied to people who were precisely one job grade higher than I was.

So if I just waited one year, produced well and received a promotion, I would be able to benefit from the Policy.

Carrot on a stick...

Shortly after this, I expressed my desire to pursue a role in another company, and *voila*! Suddenly, the Policy had changed! It had been discovered that the Policy was worded in such a way that it was at the individual manager's discretion to allow home office on a case-by-case basis.

I had read the Policy before and after. Nothing had changed. They had just realized that I was serious about my request, and decided to interpret it differently. My desire had force behind it.

II. Quit Your Bitching

How to create a powerful desire

You might be reading this and thinking that it seems absurd to be willing to leave a job over something as trivial as home office privileges.

It wasn't just about working from home. It was about one of my strongest needs at the time: autonomy.

This was 2016 – my generation had grown up with the Internet. At work, we were constantly connected – email, company phone, intra-office messenger. Days would go by without my even speaking with my boss as he was either out traveling, in meetings most of the day or grinding out late hours on some project.

I performed well, my clients were happy and I made my bosses money. My boss was the only other person working on my projects, and I was independent enough that I was handling 95% of the work.

I believe that we should act – and be treated – like responsible, independent adults who are free to make their own choices and take responsibility for their consequences.

People perform to expectations.

If we are treated like responsible adults, that's how we will act. How do you think we will act if we are treated like children?

The location in which the work is performed shouldn't particularly matter. All that matters is that the work gets done, our clients are happy and we make money.

What good reason could the company *possibly* have against occasional home office?

They will give you lots of reasons.

But if you are responsible, productive, and do a good job, there is no good reason. The only reason is control.

It is an unfortunate fact of human nature that if a person has authority over others, he will use it to exploit them for his own needs for significance and dominance.

The Stanford Prison Experiment demonstrated this with alarming clarity.

II. Quit Your Bitching

In this experiment, a group of 24 university students – selected for being the most emotionally stable and healthy in the class – was split randomly into 2 groups: prisoners and security guards. A makeshift prison was built in one of the university basements.

The experiment was to last for two weeks. Within 36 hours, the students in the security guard roles had begun psychologically abusing the prisoners. The experiment was canceled after only six days, when the conditions of the prisoners was bad enough to elicit questions from outside observers as to the morality of the experiment.

The Stanford Prison Experiment showed that people adapt to their roles. If you give someone a title and authority over someone, this person is likely to view those underneath him as being inferior, and feel empowered to treat them accordingly as a lesser being.

This same dynamic plays out among the leadership in corporate dominance hierarchies. They get a taste of status and power and suddenly they think they are somebody. They want to see their "slaves" in the office and know that they are obediently making money for them.

If you are doing home office you probably aren't as productive as you are while in office. They want to squeeze every drop of productivity out of you—never mind the fact that I routinely saw colleagues who spent half the day goofing off while in the office, and taking endless coffee and cigarette breaks.

The home office topic was merely a veneer over a deeper truth. I was bored, un-empowered, had stopped growing and wanted to try something else. I was tired of being controlled, working on someone else's clock, and deeply desired more autonomy.

They just offered me the home office carrot to entice me to stay a little longer. And it worked; I stayed 9 more months.

So again, I ask: how strong is your desire?

II. Quit Your Bitching

Since writing the first draft of this book in 2018, a paradigm-shifting event took place that may have permanently changed the way we work: a little virus known as COVID-19.

For those that were able—mainly white-collar knowledge workers—working from home became the norm during the months of quarantine.

And guess what? The work still got done.

I have spoken with a number of business leaders on this topic and nearly all of them have acknowledged that their fears about home office work were unfounded. In fact, a study done in Switzerland has indicated a productivity increase during the months of quarantine when people were working at home[2].

At publication of this book, the virus is still raging across most of the world. It has destroyed millions of jobs, crippled and ruined innumerable businesses, hobbled entire economies and generated a lot of fear.

My hope is that if there can be any positive takeaway from all this, that our attitudes toward remote work and health change for the better.

Exercise: Make a list of your values

This is a simple, but powerful exercise. On a piece of paper, simply list all of the things that you value. Think of as many things as you can. For example, here are some things that I value:

Autonomy	Peace
Love	Harmony
Contributing	Responsibility
Truth	Choice
Honesty	Seeking
Integrity	Learning
Fun	Knowledge
Connecting	Humility

---

[2] https://www.swissinfo.ch/eng/lockdown-led-to-big-jump-in-worker-productivity/45818576

II. Quit Your Bitching

Once you have your list of values:

i. Begin to rank them in order from most to least important to you. You can do this by taking each value and comparing it to each other value.

ii. If, for example, you value Autonomy over Love, put a star (*) next to Autonomy.

iii. Then compare Autonomy to the next item down the list (Contributing in my list above). If it turns out that Contributing is more important to you than Autonomy, then Contributing gets a (*).

iv. After you have gone down your list, comparing Autonomy to each value below it, go back to the 2nd value from the top (which is Love in my list). Then compare Love to the next item below it, again allocating stars, until you go all the way down through your list, comparing Love to everything below it.

v. Go back to the 3rd item from the top and continue with this until you have gone through the whole list, comparing each one against the next.

vi. Once you're finished, you should be able to rank your values from most to least important (most stars to least stars).

Now, take that Thing You Desire, and compare it against your list of values.

If it relates with some of the values near the top of your list, then you have a candidate for a really powerful desire.

II. Quit Your Bitching

Increase the intensity of your desire

Now you have your desire, ideally linked to one or more of your top values.

To really make this into a burning desire we need another ingredient:

Maintain integrity in your values.

Let's say you highly value Truth. What will you do to uphold the Truth?

If your life was a movie, how far would the hero of the story be willing to go in order to uphold this value?

Are you willing to die for it?

And if you died tomorrow, would you be happy with your life up until today and how you have lived this value?

Your values will constantly be tested. In fact, the values and desires of others will often conflict directly with yours, especially if you challenge any traditional approach or status quo.

In my own experience in the working world, the main conflict has been between Control, Autonomy and Truth.

At some level, I would have to make a choice – I would have to suppress my value of Autonomy to the Control of someone else. I would to have decide if my Truth was worth my job.

It's a compromise you make with yourself. It tells you how far you are willing to go.

For instance, although I was no longer willing to accept much of the Control of the corporate dominance hierarchy, I still live under a nation state and for the most part abide by its laws and regulations. I have given up Autonomy to some degree because of my desire to live as a more-or-less normally functional member of society.

How much are you willing to suppress your values in favor of "staying in line"?

Because the conflict will happen, and sometimes your values will get you into trouble.

In the corporate world, the Truth is often taboo.

Management prefers to extend and pretend because they are mainly evaluated on short term results.

Leadership would rather ignore the hard truths – that one of their senior managers is a micro-managing control freak that has no idea how to develop their people or win their respect. Or that top management made a bad decision that turned everybody's job into tedious drudgery (i.e. "digital transformation") and wasted millions in the process.

Leadership would rather let the low level guys resign – one after another, for years, making things increasingly inefficient and shitty with the continual knowledge drain – than take an honest look and make the hard decision.

I haven gotten into trouble for telling and acting the truth.

I realized that my last corporate job was pointless even without the endlessly encroaching, job-shittifying waves of "Digital Transformation" that took away from me the remaining modest bits of creativity that a Spreadsheet Monkey like me used to enjoy.

The problem was that I couldn't pretend. I didn't care at all about my work and everyone knew it.

I was in open rebellion against some of the nonsensical procedures they had put in place. It's hard to remain engaged when you believe that the content of your job provides no real value to anyone, and that seemingly unlimited layers of complexity and processes had been built on top of nothing in the name of pretending to add value.

I have never been able to fake emotions – you can always read them on my face.

Long story short, I made a few sloppy mistakes. No one died and it was caught and corrected before anyone was seriously impacted.

But my boss was angry at my "attitude". Even though it was clear that I had been actively disengaged for some time, nobody in management bothered to ask why, or what their own role in my lack of engagement might have been. Oh yes, they did send that "people survey" around once.

I was supposed to pretend like things were okay on the exterior and _that's_ what my boss was angry about.

Corporate incentives are also such that they often penalize Truth.

Bonuses are often paid in a certain month. Most people who intend to quit a job wait until right after their bonuses are paid before giving notice.

I knew that I was going to leave and I gave the leadership 5 months additional verbal notice than was contractually obligated, so that they had sufficient time to look for a replacement.

I thought I was doing right by them, doing what was good for the business. My reward? No bonus. Because I told them before the bonuses were paid out, I got nothing.

Companies also sometimes measure overtime as part of your performance. Does that make sense? The more hours you work, the better you have performed?

I was fast, efficient, and honest with my hours, which meant that they didn't need to pay me overtime and I saved them money. Penalty.

How many people do you know in the corporate world who do next to nothing, but spend a lot of their time talking up their jobs to make it seem like they are busier or more important than they really are?

I learned a valuable lesson that is true of some organizations:

Pretend, extend, and get promoted.

Tell the truth at your own risk.

Sorry, I went off on a bit of a tangent there.

The moral was, at least for me, my value for Truth did not fit into that particular organization, as too much of the structure was built on avoiding the truth.

I merely wanted to illustrate an example of where your values can take you if you hold onto them strongly and follow them to their logical conclusion.

Look again at your list of values.

How prepared are you to *really* live them? What are you willing to sacrifice?

III.
Decide Where You Want to Go

Maybe you've decided that the culture at your workplace is no longer in line with your values, or that your job isn't meeting your needs.

Maybe you want to go back to school, start your own business, become a freelance consultant, join the digital nomads, teach languages abroad, become a blogger, or engage in one of the countless other endeavors that exist outside the corporate ladder climbing world.

What do you do next?

Do you quit?

The answer is that it depends entirely on your needs.

If you have a high need for certainty, then you probably shouldn't quit. You are used to a structure, and you could struggle if you suddenly found yourself without a routine or a place to go everyday. You might suffer from high blood pressure, anxiety, insomnia or even panic attacks.

Hell, even for me it was quite an emotional struggle at times, and I have a pretty low need for certainty.

The safer and less stressful route is to build up something on the side until it starts generating income for you. This is also a good test of how dedicated or passionate you are for the project.

What are you willing to give up in order to get what you want?

Are you willing to give up all your free time? Your early mornings, evenings, and weekends?

Are you willing to invest time and money learning new skills and use your vacations to attend the training that you need in order to get you where you need to go, instead of lying on a beach drinking daiquiris?

Are you ready to give up watching Netflix and playing video games?

Will you give up your 4 nights out a week?

Accept these sacrifices in advance.

The extent to which you are willing to do the above is a good indicator of how successful you will be in your new endeavor.

If you find that 3 months into starting the thing, your leisure hours start to creep back in, odds are you don't have enough passion for your project to see it through.

Good thing you didn't quit that job.

Thomas Edison once said:

> "Genius is 1% inspiration and 99% perspiration".

Follow-through is everything.

If you're able to balance your job until your new venture takes off, you will find the transition into "freedom" to be much smoother and less stressful.

On the other hand, it has also been said:

> "There are two great motivators in life: inspiration and desperation."
> Robert Hollis

And desperation is probably the greater motivator.

Nothing will light a hotter fire under your ass than when you're no longer getting paychecks and watching your meager savings slowly fizzle out like a dying candle flame.

This is when your true grit, your hustle will show up. You'll work 18 hour days because you *have* to. It's about survival now.

This makes you creative. When your survival is on the line, *you will find a way*. It may not be the way you imagined, but you will survive.

Life supports life.

> "Nature loves courage. You make the commitment and nature will respond to that commitment by removing impossible obstacles. Dream the impossible dream and the world will not grind you under, it will lift you up. This is the trick. This is what all these teachers and philosophers who really counted, who really touched the alchemical gold, this is what they understood. This is the shamanic dance in the waterfall. This is how magic is done. By hurling yourself into the abyss and discovering it's a feather bed."
> Terence McKenna

When I moved to Switzerland with my wife in 2012, we were jobless for nearly a year.

The only work experience I had was as an English teacher and translator, and in Switzerland they expected you to have four year university degrees in anything in order to be able to work in that field. I had experience but not the degrees, which apparently counted for nothing. I had an economics and business degree but no real experience in business.

We had a comfortable safety net at first. We stayed with my aunt and uncle, who grew apples and pears. This covered most of our expenses because we helped them with farming in exchange for room and board. They lived 40 minutes by car from Lucerne, the nearest city. We didn't have a car.

For 2 months nothing happened. We stagnated. We saved on our costs, but nothing progressed. Not one job interview.

We were politely asked to leave. The safety net was gone. We had no choice but to move into the only place that would take us: a sublease in a shared tenement apartment in the ass end of Lucerne, right at the city's edge along the train tracks.

Our flatmates were a sporadically employed Dutch waiter who drank and chain-smoked all day long in the living area when he wasn't working (which was most of the time), and a Vietnamese student who smelled strongly of the potatoes and onions that she stored in her bedroom instead of the kitchen.

The other residents of the building were on social assistance. An alcoholic lived above us who sang drunkenly and loudly into the late hours each night. Our neighbor across the hall was a popular drug dealer with a continuous flow of clients in and out from the street.

The communal shower was in the kitchen. My wife and I shared a poorly heated 14 m² room where we also took all of our meals, because though it was only October it was already winter and the apartment windows were kept closed, which meant that the living area was always filled with a thick, stagnant smoke cloud that seeped into our clothes, hair and skin.

I will always remember my 30th birthday. October 27, 2012.

We had just moved into that apartment 2 weeks before. We were having a quiet dinner at a modestly-priced Mexican restaurant across the street, strangers in a new city, when it began to snow heavily.

Switzerland will suck through your savings in no time. We weren't even sure how – we thought we were living very frugally. We saved on alcohol by buying double strong 8.8% alcoholic beer at CHF 0.88 a can and splitting it with lemon soda. Money just seemed to evaporate.

We were cold and alone, our cash was running out, and each dusting of snow in the following days further extinguished our hopes and dreams.

This was not the way things were supposed to turn out.

We only had enough money to get us through Christmas.

We made an agreement that night: that if we didn't make it by the end of the year, we would have to leave. We didn't know where to.

I started canvassing the streets with renewed vigor.

For every job that I applied to, I physically went to the office and presented my CV in person.

I met as many people as I could.

I followed every lead that popped up. Waiter jobs, bartender jobs, renting out e-bikes, anything.

Eventually I started to get return calls.

III. Decide Where You Want to Go

These led to further meetings and interviews. I went to the interviews in my solitary cigarette smoke-infused suit, hoping my interviewers wouldn't notice the smell.

End of November. My spirits were high, things were looking positive but I still had nothing concrete and time was running out.

Then, in the very last week before Christmas, I received a job offer paying CHF 80,000 per year, starting on January 3rd. Easily double the highest salary I had ever earned.

The following day, as if by magic, I received a completely unexpected phone call from a friend of a friend. A beautiful apartment with an unobstructed view of the lake and the snow-capped Alps had become available and we could move in immediately!!

This is the magic of *despermism* – desperation combined with optimism.

If you keep your spirits high, your goal sharply in focus, you have a burning desire for it and you keep trying, life will support you. Energies will coalesce around you and deliver you what you need, at the time you need it.

If you are aligned – in line with your Why and following it with passion, feeling good most of the time, staying optimistic and open toward opportunity and others, saying "YES!" to anything that comes into your experience – life will catch you. It will help you out.

There is an unseen force at work. Call it energy, vibration, God, the Universe, whatever you believe. It responds to your emotions and subconscious requests and will materialize people, circumstances and events into your experience that push you forward toward your desires.

Often this will happen when you are at the bottom, you've put in everything you've got, and have nothing left to lose.

The main problem with quitting is the timing.

If you time it wrong – if your journey takes longer than you had planned and your money runs out sooner than you had expected – you could end up right where you left off, or back in your parents' basement, or in a van down by the river.

As a general rule: You will <u>ALWAYS</u> underestimate how much money you'll need.

Then you'll run out and have to take another job, which could delay your plans as you save up more money until you are able to make another run for it. Or maybe the stress of it all will make you give it up altogether.

But in my opinion, this is all part of the journey. There is no avoiding the pitfalls when swinging through the jungle. The pitfalls are a test to see how much you want it.

Maybe you do run out of money, and have to take some odd job to bridge your way through it. You'll find yourself in a new environment with new people, maybe in a new country, and this will be stimulating.

There isn't one answer that works for everyone. You just have to understand what kind of person you are and what you can manage given your needs and set of responsibilities, and decide how you want to go about it.

You can always get more money.

You can never get more time.

At least until the robots come.

But by then we will hopefully have universal basic income, else we're all fucked anyway.

III. Decide Where You Want to Go

The only way to gain perspective on an environment is to leave it

This holds true for all things: families, relationships, friendships, institutions, religions, corporations, cultures, nation-states.

Prior to joining the corporate world at the seasoned age of 30, I had already been working outside of it for many years. I had drifted around Asia for 7 years working an assortment of jobs. I had been an English teacher, freelance editor/translator, even a fake priest. I had had full time jobs, part time jobs, and substitute jobs – anything that came up and suited my needs at the time.

I never made much money doing this, but it was always enough. Except for the fake priest gig and my 2 years working in the Japanese public school system, I never had to dress up. I wore shorts, T-shirts and sandals every day. Even in public school I didn't *really* dress up – I worked in slacks and a button-down shirt. No ties – ever.

Not that there's anything wrong with dressing up. I just wasn't used to it, and didn't particularly care for it.

It gave me a unique perspective. I was totally new to having a 9-5 corporate job and wearing nice clothes to work in a fixed location among others who had gone to the same tailor that apparently sold the same color suits and ties.

It was a strange experience at first. Most of my colleagues dressed and acted the same. There was a corporate uniform code of conduct and a uniformity of political opinion (left-leaning, pro-globalization). If you wanted to create an awkward silence at lunch, you had only to say that you thought some of U.S. presidential candidate Trump's opinions had merit.

We had people of different color and nationality. On paper, our team was very global – of the 60 or so employees, we easily represented 20 countries.

But where was the diversity of opinion?

Conversations tended to revolve around work difficulties and escape – asking about the weekend or that next vacation. It seemed as though most people didn't really want to be there.

As I continued to observe my environment, it began to dawn on me how this could happen.

Most people in that environment had followed the Standard Path: 12 years of public education, 4-year degree from a liberal arts university, internship, and direct insertion onto the corporate ladder at the age of 22.

You probably received your primary education in a public school, like I did. Unfortunately, most public schools are not really about learning or creativity. In fact they may be the worst places for this.

How can you stimulate a passion for learning in children if the only goal is to get them to memorize facts to repeat on an exam?

How can you delve deeply into a subject if you only have 40-60 minutes to work on it before you need to race off to the next class?

How can you support a diversity of learning approaches and styles by teaching a set curriculum to all students in the same way?

How can you engage a student with genius and a genuine interest in learning, when you have to tailor the class to the slowest student, to ensure that she gets through it and passes the standard exam?

In public school, you learn mainly to be punctual and how to be a good, productive member of society. Generally you are taught the Government Approved Version of History. Everything is set up to prepare you for the Standard Path described above.

As an adult, you are surrounded by other large sized children who have been "schooled" into more or less the same model of the world: get into a good university, land a secure corporate job, climb the ladder, retire.

When you're in the system, you risk becoming blind and losing perspective.

Your environment shapes your thinking.

The ideas, feelings and energies of your bosses and colleagues merge with yours. You – being a new entrant into the workplace – are eager to fit in, so you conform. You take on the same life goals (become the boss someday, chase promotions), wear the same clothes, pursue the same hobbies (golf, assembling a collection of fine red wines), buy the house, settle down.

We conform to our environment over time. It's necessary for human survival, to feel connection, and to advance within a specific hierarchy.

III. Decide Where You Want to Go

The same applies to culture and national identity.

We all have to go through public and social education in order to function normally in society. But as adults, if we want to become aware we must spend time un-learning much of what we were taught in order to understand ourselves and forge our own unique paths.

When I was 22 I left the United States for Japan, and I was fortunate enough to have a job that afforded me plenty of free time to read and investigate world history and politics, and be surrounded by other young people from different countries and with different backgrounds.

I experienced a completely different way to live life. It exposed me to a huge diversity of new ideas and ways of thinking. It was only then that I could examine my culture from afar, see some of the problems with it, and understand why I felt unhappy with certain aspects of it.

I don't mean to suggest that your environment is "bad" by definition. Nothing is either good or bad.

Your unhappiness could stem from a lack of perspective about how good you have it now – in this sense, practicing poverty and living in an unfamiliar situation may make you more appreciative of the comfort and security you now enjoy.

What about family and friends?

You've probably heard the following quote:

> *"5 years from now, your income will be the average of that of your 5 best friends."*

As with any environment, your social circle will influence and re-inforce your opinions, hobbies, values, and beliefs about the world.

If you find that your friends are not supportive of the person you want to become, you will need to change them.

III. Decide Where You Want to Go

This will happen organically as you begin to live out your new values and beliefs. Your former relationships will begin to drop away as you outgrow them, and new friendships will form in their place. You will join different clubs and societies of like-minded people that share your values and will support you along your path.

This step is painful yet necessary. You simply cannot afford to have people around you who do not support you. If you are to build a superstructure of your life, you need to have a solid foundation of relationships around you.

When it comes to family, there is no easy solution.

Life is an unfair race and you don't get to choose your starting place.

If your parents were abusive and addicted to drugs or alcohol, you lived in the slums and all your friends had similar backgrounds, the odds are stacked heavily against you from the beginning.

If you had truly abusive parents then you need to try to drop them from your life.

If your parents are merely stuck in self-destructive thinking patterns, the best you can do is limit your exposure to them and see if you can help them change their thinking over time. You cannot do this through argumentation, but only by demonstrating to them by example.

III. Decide Where You Want to Go

Your beliefs are a choice

The reason we have organized religions in the world is simple:

Civilizations that were backed by a fanatical belief in a higher power conquered the civilizations that didn't have that belief.

It is much easier to organize a force of people to risk their lives in the name of conquest and territorial expansion if that conquest is backed by a divine power, a belief that they are fighting in the name of a God, and that their lives were to be sacrificed toward a higher purpose.

Sure, lords could punish the peasants if they didn't fight. They could promise them some of the spoils of war.

But as we now know, fear and greed will only motivate a person so far.

If you really want to get someone motivated and inspired to accomplish a goal, you have to give them a deep sense of purpose: tap into their most deeply-held beliefs, and help them meet the most fundamental need of all: the need for meaning.

We form our beliefs by attaching significance to things that happen in our lives. This is how we develop our "story", the narrative we tell ourselves about what is "true for me".

An event only needs to be repeated once or twice for it to become a belief.

For instance, you take a taxi across town. The driver is Indian and he is rude to you.

A few days later, you take another taxi ride. This driver, who is different, is also Indian and is also rude to you.

Just from these two experiences you might already form the belief: *Indians are rude*.

This is now one of your rudimentary beliefs.

Similarly, if you grew up in a rough neighborhood and experienced violence, deception and theft, you may form the belief that people are generally dishonest and not to be trusted.

III. Decide Where You Want to Go

In grammar school, if you struggled with math and your math teacher didn't know how to adapt their teaching style to your learning style, and you didn't do well on your exams, you may have developed the belief that you're "just not good at math" or that you're "stupid".

Many geniuses of their art were "taught" at an early age that they "couldn't cut it".

Michael Jordan was cut from his high school basketball team.

Albert Einstein failed his university entrance exam the first time.

Stephen King submitted the manuscript for *Carrie* 31 times before it was accepted.

Belief was the only thing that kept them going.

The good news is that your beliefs can be changed by changing your focus.

You can see the good in the world, or the evil.

You can believe that you are intelligent and resourceful, or stupid and useless.

You can choose to believe in yourself.

III. Decide Where You Want to Go

Exercise: Beliefs

Print out the table below (or write in it directly if reading a paper copy).

In the columns under the heading "my current beliefs", fill in everything you currently believe about people and the world (global beliefs) and about yourself and your own abilities (personal beliefs). Anything and everything goes here.

A global belief could be something like "People are generally good". A personal belief could be, "I am a good friend".

Another set of beliefs could be, "You must be smart to succeed" (Global) and "I am not very smart" (Personal).

Once you have done that, look over your list.

Which beliefs are serving you?

Which beliefs are blocking you from financial, relationship, health, or career success?

Identify those beliefs that are no longer serving you.

Take each of those negative beliefs and write out its opposite into the respective column under the subheading "Beliefs I want to have". For instance, if you wrote "I am bad at math", you could change it to "I can improve in math if I really apply myself".

The trick is to word it in a way to make it believable to you; writing, "I am a math genius" might not work if you currently believe you are bad at math.

Then for each of the beliefs you want to have, see if you can find an example from your life experience which supports it.

III. Decide Where You Want to Go

MY CURRENT BELIEFS		BELIEFS I WANT TO HAVE	
Global beliefs	**Personal beliefs**	**Global beliefs [actualized]**	**Personal beliefs [adjusted]**
You need to be smart to be financially successful.	I am not very smart.	Financial success depends more on persistence than intelligence.	Though I may not be a genius, I am reasonably smart and have common sense. I can also be hard working and persistent, which is 99% of success.

The nature of reality

In order to be the Masters of our Universe, it's worthwhile to try to understand how our Universe works.

What is it made of?

Let's begin by considering the most famous of mathematical equations:

$E = mC^2$

$E = energy$

$m = mass$

$C = the\ speed\ of\ light$

We all learned this in school. We were told that it was derived by the most incredible genius in recent human memory.

But did you ever stop to consider what this actually means?

It basically says that mass (matter) and energy are interchangeable – that if you take a piece of matter and make it move really fast, it becomes energy.

Another way to interpret this is to say that matter moving at the speed of light is pure energy.

Whereas matter that is moving very slowly can be thought of as "frozen" energy.

Think about water, and the states of matter it goes through.

When water is at very low energy – its molecules are stabilized into crystals and barely moving at all – it is ice. A solid block of matter.

If you heat it up – in other words, apply energy and cause its molecules to move more rapidly – it becomes liquid water.

Continue to add energy, the molecules move ever more quickly and the water becomes steam, and evaporates away into the air.

It's difficult to conceptualize matter as frozen energy, but this is the principle upon which nuclear physics was built – slamming particles (matter) into each other at high speed to convert the matter into a massive release of energy.

It gets even stranger when we stop to consider what matter is actually made of. We are told that matter is made of molecules, which is a group of bound atoms.

III. Decide Where You Want to Go

Remember this from school?

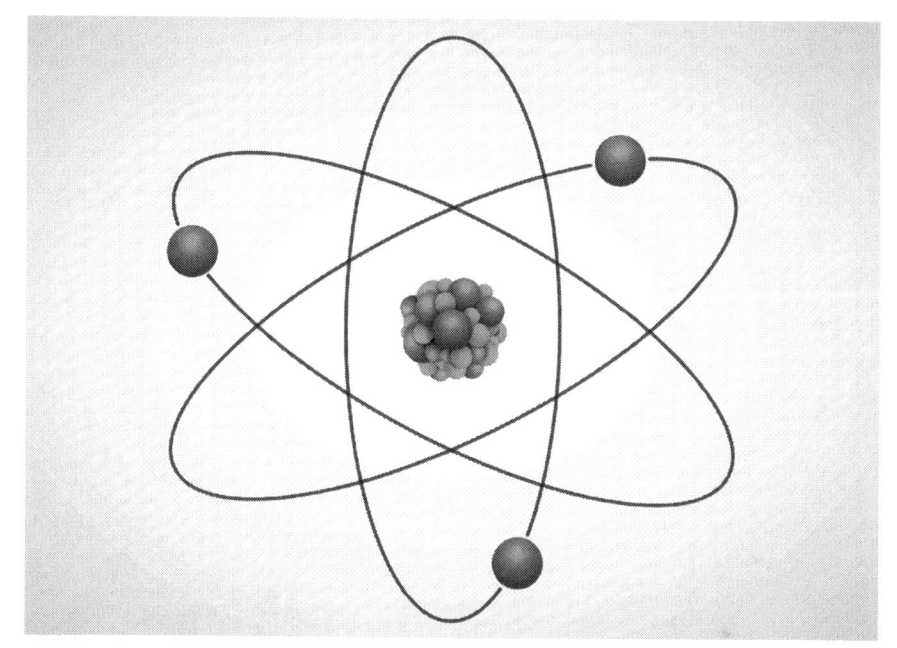

Figure 1

We imagine the atom with the nucleus like a sun, and the electron orbiting the nucleus like a planet. However, modern science indicates to us that this is not really what an atom looks like at all.

Scientists have still not really been able to "see" an atom, but the newest information suggests that it looks more like this:

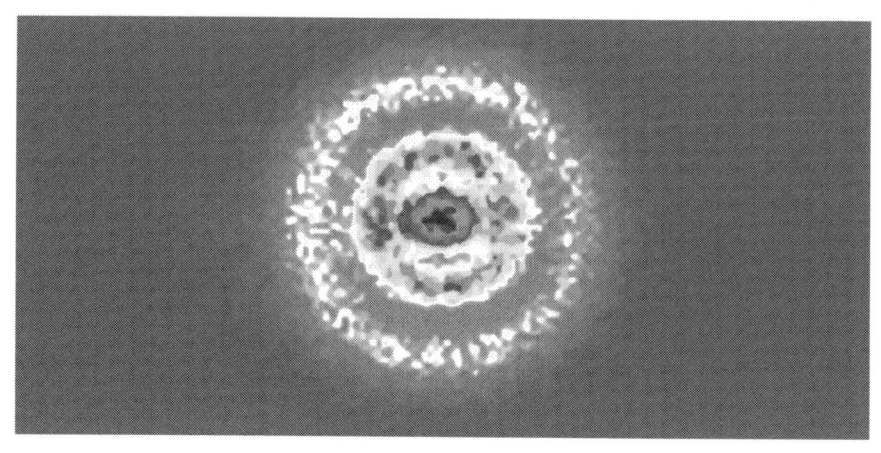

Figure 2

III. Decide Where You Want to Go

It has a nucleus (central area), but the electrons do not orbit neatly in fixed locations.

In fact, an electron is never really in a fixed location – it inhabits a "probability cloud", which means that it has a certain probability of being anywhere within a specific region.

In Figure 2 you can see the probability cloud in the outer ring – it has bright and dark areas. The bright areas indicate areas of greater probability that you will find an electron if you look there.

Figure 2 still shows a more or less circular orbit, as the image was taken as if looking "from above".

Electrons orbits actually appear in unintuitive shapes:

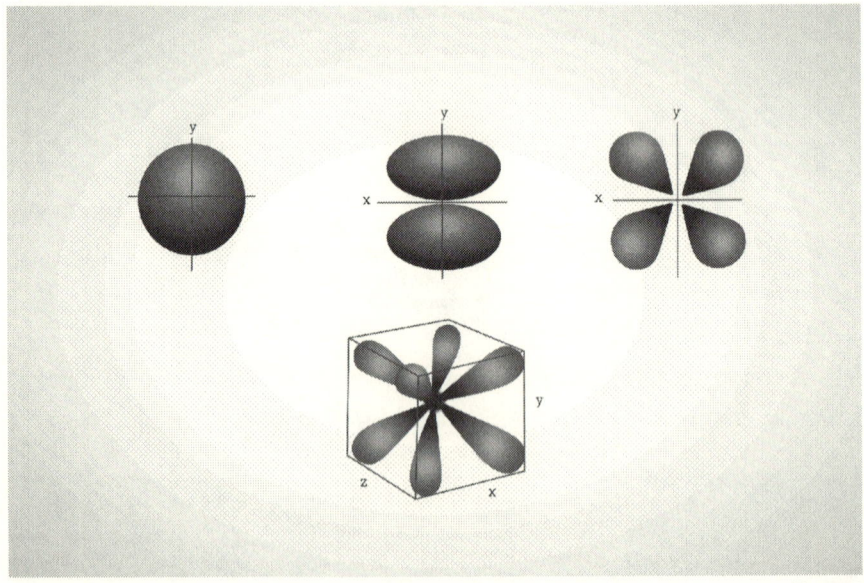

Figure 3

Far from being a circular orbit, it can be more of a sphere, with bulging areas in which the probability of an electron being there is higher.

What is freakish about all this is that the electron only appears in a fixed location <u>when it is measured.</u>

Until the electron is actually measured, it only exists as a probability wave. That means it is both everywhere and nowhere along its probability cloud until

III. Decide Where You Want to Go

some action causes its location to be "computed", and it appears at a particular point in space and time.

This phenomenon is called *particle-wave duality*.

It turns out that *any* particle or piece of matter – electron, atom, even molecules! – also has the properties of a wave. A wave is a form of energy that has an amplitude and frequency just like a radio wave.

This means that the fundamental building blocks of every solid object that we see – protons, neutrons, electrons, and the dozens of even smaller particles they are made of – are actually energy waves spread out over a potential area of localization.

They only become "particles" once we measure them and the 'wave function collapses'–in other words, it 'decides' to exist as a physical object at a specific location.

This is true of **all** matter, and this feature of the particle-wave duality of matter is the foundation of all of quantum physics.

> *"Anyone who is not shocked by quantum physics has not understood it... Everything we call real is made of things that cannot be regarded as real"*
> *Niels Bohr*

If that isn't weird enough for you, here is another fact that will melt your mind: 99.9999999% of your body is empty space.

According to physicist Ali Sundermeier:

"If the nucleus were the size of a peanut, the atom would be about the size of a baseball stadium. If we lost all the dead space inside our atoms, we would each be able to fit into a particle of dust, and the entire human race would fit into the volume of a sugar cube."

But if we are mostly empty, why do we have mass?

Most scientists believe that almost all of our mass is actually energy – specifically, the energy produced by the sub-subatomic particles like quarks and gluons that use energy to bind together and create protons, neutrons and electrons.

It bears repeating: Nearly all of our physical mass is actually energy.

Apparently, it is not quite true that we are "empty".

Scientists have interesting ways of describing this "empty" space – probability clouds, wave functions, invisible quantum energy fields in which particles can wink in and out of existence all the time.

And the electron, because it is actually a wave, is somehow simultaneously "everywhere" inside the atom. Wherever you touch, there the electrons go.

The fact is we never actually "touch" anything – the sensation of touch we feel is really the electromagnetic force of some electrons pressing against other electrons.

And you thought your life was boring.

III. Decide Where You Want to Go

Everything is connected

Not only is everything we see, touch, and feel mostly empty space and energy – everything also seems to be energetically connected to everything else.

Where exactly does your body end?

You might say that your body's physical limit is your hair or skin, but then you are breathing and exhaling air, emitting wonderful gases, heat, electromagnetic waves, dandruff, pheromones, germs, bacteria, and other things.

These are collections of "your" atoms that then interact with the universe around them.

The idea that matter can be connected across space is called Entanglement – or what Einstein famously called, "spooky action at a distance".

In quantum physics, particle-waves can be thought of as being in a "neutral" state.

While an electron sits comfortably in its probability cloud undetected, it is neither "here" nor "there" until it is measured. Until it is detected it is both "here" AND "there" simultaneously.

For instance, a pair of photons (light particles) have opposite polarity; let's call them plus (+) and minus (-), just like a magnet has "North" and "South" magnetism.

Before measurement, the photons are in a neutral state like the electrons in the probability cloud: both (+) and (-) simultaneously.

When one photon is observed and discovered to have minus (-) polarity, the other photon instantly reveals itself to have plus (+) polarity, and this regardless of the amount of separation between them.

Einstein referred to this phenomenon as "spooky action at a distance" because the amount of distance between the photons had no effect on the amount of time it took for the other photon to "choose" its polarity. It happened instantaneously.

This violates a fundamental principle of physics, as the amount of time it should take for the "information" from the one photon to travel to the other should be no faster than the amount of time it would take for light to travel across the same distance.

This "spooky action at a distance" is called quantum entanglement.

The fact that the particles "communicate" to each other like this implies one of two things:

- → That there is a speed faster than light, but this invalidates much of modern physics as the speed of light is a constant and nothing can travel faster than light. Or:
- → Particles and energy are somehow connected to each other

Einstein never fully accepted this, but so far it has been validated by over 50 years of experimentation.

III. Decide Where You Want to Go

Superstring Theory

> *"The day science begins to study non-physical phenomena, it will make more progress in one decade than in all the previous centuries of its existence... If you want to find the secrets of the universe, think in terms of energy, frequency and vibration."*
> Nikola Tesla

To date, the most promising attempt in physics to unify the various interpretations of reality is called Superstring Theory.

Though superstrings have not yet been observed experimentally, Superstring Theory says that the most elementary thing in the universe – smaller than protons, electrons, quarks, gluons, and everything else – is a vibrating string. These strings vibrate at different frequencies to produce the different components of matter.

To simplify the idea, think of the superstrings like a guitar string.

If a superstring (or combination of superstrings) vibrates the note "A" it is a proton. The note "E" is an electron, "D" is a photon (light), and so forth.

Imagine that the entire universe is made of a nearly infinite number of vibrating strings. The different vibrations produce the different physical objects we see and the energies and waves we can measure. These strings are all connected to each other in a co-active web of infinite complexity.

Imagine now invisible vibrating strings as the basis of your whole body and coming from you out into space in all possible directions, connected to every other object, person, thought, and energy via its underlying strings. This is how everything is connected; much like an infinite spiderweb. One movement of the thread of your thinking thus reverberates throughout the whole universe.

The idea of vibrating strings underlying creation is not new.

Ancient cultures have posited similar interpretations of the universe.

Native Americans believe that a Spider Grandmother weaved nature into being and that this spider preceded all of existence [3].

---

[3] https://en.wikipedia.org/wiki/Spider_Grandmother

Archaeologists have discovered wall reliefs within pyramids from the ancient culture of Teotihuacan depicting a spider woman functioning as the goddess of creation.

The Great Mother as a spider also figures into the mythology of tribes in Cameroon and other areas of Africa.

Perhaps the ancients intuitively understood this subtle and invisible connection between all things, and modern science is only now beginning to provide the physical evidence.

Thoughts are things

Anywhere there is a nerve cell, there is electricity. Nerve impulses are mostly electrical signals.

And anywhere you have an electrical signal, you have an electromagnetic field around it.

Your brain is the part of your body that is the most densely concentrated with nerve cells. These nerve cells in your brain communicate with each other to create brain waves, which can be detected with standard medical equipment.

These electromagnetic impulses generated by your brain's nerve cells as you think a thought are governed by the same laws of quantum physics as all of the particles we have hitherto discussed: particle-wave duality, entanglement, vibrating strings of energy.

When you think, an electrical impulse is generated, and this can be measured.

Like all the rest of matter, thoughts are energy.

This further implies that our thoughts are subject to the same law of quantum entanglement as all other matter.

III. Decide Where You Want to Go

Mind over matter

There is some evidence that your thoughts can directly affect matter.

The most well-known experiments are those conducted by Mr. Masuru Emoto in Japan, who experimented with intention and water. These experiments were mentioned in the movie *What the Bleep Do We Know*.

His experiments reportedly showed that the transmission of positively-intended thoughts – thoughts of love, appreciation, and beauty – toward jars of water produced aesthetically more pleasing water crystals than in water toward which no such intention was sent.

His results are interesting, though there is some controversy about his methodology (mostly that we don't know fully what his methodology was).

Mr. Emoto has done similar experiments with rice sitting in jars filled with water. You can find these on YouTube. He has 3 jars of rice. To the first jar, he sends thoughts of love and appreciation. He sends hate to the 2nd jar, and leaves the 3rd jar alone.

In his Youtube experiment, the rice in the jar that received love turned out fine, whereas the rice in the other two jars turned black or moldy.

What makes this experiment interesting is that it is easy to reproduce in your home. However, results have been mixed – some people have reported duplicating Mr. Emoto's findings, whereas for others, nothing observable happened to any of the jars of rice.

There have been other studies into whether our thoughts and intentions are able to directly affect matter:

- → Frontiers and their study of pre-cognition, the human ability to predict events up to 1-10 seconds into the future [4]
- → Princeton study on consciousness and its impact on Random Number Generators [5]
- → US Government-sponsored studies on Psychokinesis [6]

---

4 https://www.frontiersin.org/articles/10.3389/fnhum.2014.00146/full
5 http://noosphere.princeton.edu/
6 https://fas.org/sgp/eprint/teleport.pdf

III. Decide Where You Want to Go

Though these studies are fascinating, I wouldn't go so far as to call them conclusive evidence of the ability of your mind to directly affect matter.

But your mind can certainly affect reality *indirectly*.

Your thoughts are the basis of your emotional state and your attitude. These in turn affect how you project yourself into the world and all the non-verbal signals you give others – your willingness to smile and be approached, your level of confidence, how you treat others and how you expect to be treated.

You communicate your standards with your attitude.

This then influences the actions you take and the way people respond to you, which will result in a new outcome.

If your thoughts are focused and optimistic and this generates feelings of happiness and energy, it is that much more likely that you will reach out to someone and initiate contact and they will respond positively to you.

This contact could end up helping you in unexpected ways, make a new connection, or become a new friend, mentor or business associate that can have a huge impact on your future.

Life Coach Brooke Castillo calls this feedback loop The Model.

Take a while and let this sink in, as this will form the basis for your re-birth. It is simple but extremely profound. Once you fully understand, integrate and master The Model in your daily life, you will never be the victim again, and you will create magic in your life.

The Model

> *"Life is 10% what happens to you and 90% how you react to it"*
> Charles R. Swindoll

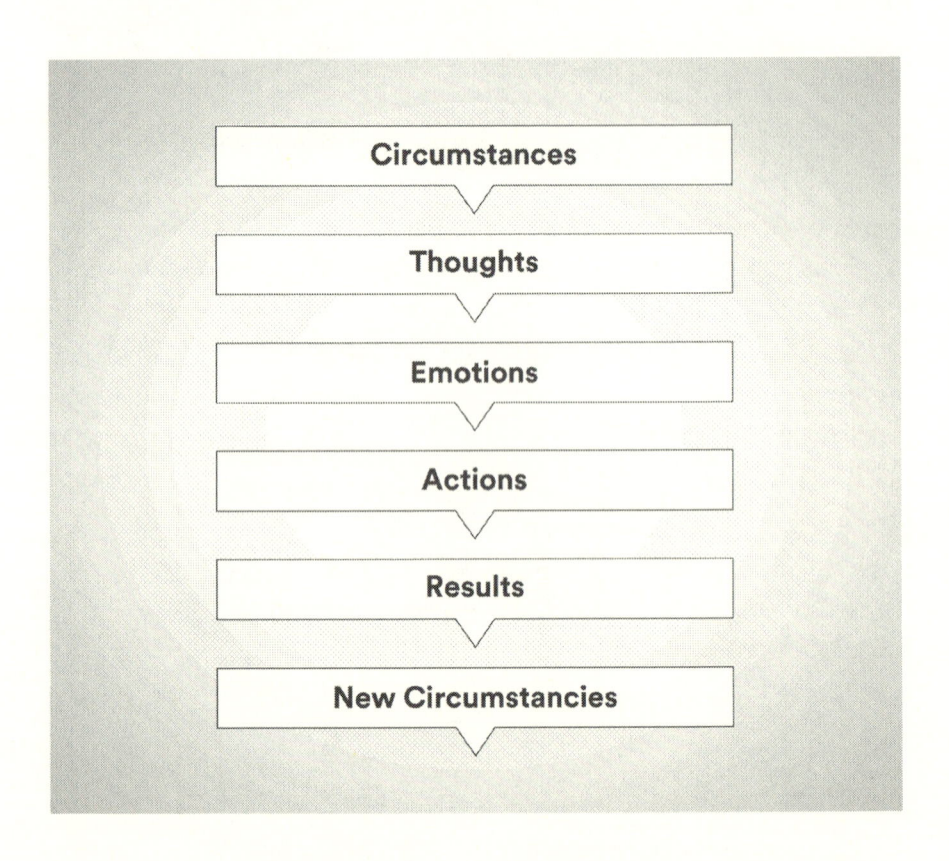

Circumstances
↓
Thoughts
↓
Emotions
↓
Actions
↓
Results
↓
New Circumstancies
↓

You think thoughts in response to your circumstances. These thoughts generate in you a certain emotional state. You take a specific action arising from that emotional state, which produces a result and a new set of circumstances, and the cycle repeats.

Your pathway in life can in this way be traced back to the neural pathways in your brain.

III. Decide Where You Want to Go

If you respond to circumstances with negative thinking, you will feel bad, take unproductive or detrimental action which will generate new circumstances that are energetically similar to the emotions you started with.

In this way, your thoughts create your reality. Your reality is fully subject to interpretation, and the main element you can control is how you think about things.

Two Wolves: a Cherokee legend

An old Cherokee is teaching his grandson about life.

"A fight is going on inside me," he said to the boy.

"It is a terrible fight and it is between two wolves.

One is evil — he is anger, envy, sorrow, regret, greed, arrogance, self-pity, guilt, resentment, inferiority, lies, false pride, superiority, and ego."

He continued, "The other is good — he is joy, peace, love, hope, serenity, humility, kindness, benevolence, empathy, generosity, truth, compassion, and faith.

The same fight is going on inside you — and inside every other person, too."

The grandson thought about it for a minute and then asked his grandfather, "Which wolf will win?"

The old Cherokee simply replied, "The one you feed."

III. Decide Where You Want to Go

The Law of Attraction

> *"You are a vibrational being living in a vibrational universe"*
> *Abraham Hicks*

You might have heard of the book and film *The Secret*.

I have some reservations about the book, but *The Secret* was really the first book to popularize the Law of Attraction around the world, and it was my first exposure to this concept.

The Law of Attraction basically states that *like attracts like*.

If we go back to our previous section on physics, we learned that the most promising theory to unite all of physics – Superstring theory – is premised on the idea that all of matter is comprised of strings that vibrate at different frequencies.

This implies that everything in the universe – including you – is vibrational in nature.

I ask you to suspend your disbelief for a moment and think of yourself as a collection of vibrating energies, rather than a hunk of meat, blood, bacteria and various odors.

According to the Law of Attraction, you will attract circumstances around you which match the predominant vibration you are emitting.

What do we mean by "emitting vibration?"

We mean your thoughts, emotions and intentions.

We are able to calibrate the type of electrical signal that we emit with our brains. The higher the quality or consciousness of our thought, the higher the emitted frequency. We can also focus our thinking for longer periods of time to emit sustained signals of the same frequency.

Imagine all your potential futures to be like the wave function of an electron that is still in its probability cloud. It has not happened yet, so it is in a neutral state of existing. It is pure potential.

III. Decide Where You Want to Go

With your mind, you can influence which reality your future will 'collapse its wave function' into by focusing and directing your thoughts to visualize the kind of future you want.

Whatever "vibration" of energy you put out into the world in terms of thoughts, emotions and intentions will be attracted back to you. Like attracts like.

In this way, you exercise the God-like creative aspect of Man – you can create your future.

We are doing this all the time, and you've been doing it since you were born. Think of life as a grand play of incomprehensible complexity. Each person is creating their own reality, and is simultaneously an actor in the realities of everyone else.

Why and how the Law of Attraction works is a mystery. But it does work. And you can use it to create the future you want.

With an important caveat...

An important distinction in how the Law of Attraction works

In my opinion there are two key ingredients to the Law of Attraction that are not sufficiently emphasized in *The Secret*: belief and action.

Dreams Exercise

Let's do a quick exercise.

Step 1:

Make a list of everything you want out of life, big or small, tangible or intangible. No limits! Any crazy dream goes here. Imagine that money was no object, and that you knew you couldn't fail.

Anything at all.

Go ahead and make your list, and describe each item in detail.

Step 2:

After you have completed your list, take another look through each item.

For each item ask yourself the following question:

"How confident am I that I can have or achieve this within 1 year?"

Then give each item on the list a ranking from 1 to 10.

A 10 means "definitely happening", and 1 means "not a chance".

Do this now.

Step 3:

Each goal or dream should now have a number next to it.

Look at your list again.

Now drop every item that you've ranked lower than 8.

It's not going to happen for you.

Why?

III. Decide Where You Want to Go

Because you do not have sufficient belief that you can achieve it.

You should only focus on the goals that you've ranked an 8 or higher. These are the goals that are most likely to excite you, as they hopefully generate a strong positive emotion, and feel like they are within your grasp. You can create a healthy obsession about them.

<u>The Law of Attraction does not work for goals that you do not believe in.</u>

The process is self-defeating. You are emitting a positive intention toward a thing, but you are simultaneously sending out a counter-intention that you can't have it.

So you must begin with goals that you believe to be achievable.

Once some of those initially smaller things begin to materialize, your confidence will build and you will have more belief that you can attain some of the goals you had previously ranked below 8.

This is the success snowball effect.

Worry and self-doubt are forms of counter-intention.

When you worry, you are setting a negative goal; you are imagining the worst possible outcome. The intention and counter-intention neutralize each other, and nothing happens.

Later, I will give you some strategies and suggestions to overcome worry and self-doubt, but for now just keep this in your mind: avoid all goals which cause you excessive worry or doubt.

III. Decide Where You Want to Go

The 3 Step Process to manifest your desires

The process to activate the Law of Attraction and manifest your dreams and desires is simple.

There are only 3 steps:

1. Asking
2. Allowing
3. Receiving

This is essentially the same process as described in the Abraham-Hicks books like *Ask and it is Given*.

Simple doesn't necessarily mean easy; there are a lot of nuances that make it work.

Step One: Asking

By Ask, I mean "put your intention out into the world". In other words, use your mind to send out the thought or emotion related to the goal or dream that you have.

This is where you communicate what you want to the "universe", "God", "life energy" or whatever you want to call the mysterious force that seems to run the show from behind the curtains.

Asking is mainly done by visualizing your desired outcome:

Go back to the list you made and take one of the goals you've ranked 8, 9, or 10.

Visualize it as clearly as possible. Play it like a movie in your mind, a movie in which you are the hero.

What are the sights you see? Sounds? Smells? How do you feel in your body?

Add color to the vision. Make it bright and close to you, clear and in focus.

Add sounds and hear them clearly around you.

Feel the sensations you would feel if you were actually there – the sand between your toes if you are on a beach, for example. Or the feel and smell of lying in cut grass in a field on a warm summer night.

III. Decide Where You Want to Go

Visualize every little detail and make it as real as you can.

Try to feel the emotion you would feel if it had already manifested in your life.

Play this movie in your mind as often as possible, for at least 2 minutes each time.

When doing this visualization, pay careful attention to your emotions.

If you feel bad, like you don't deserve it, you are operating from a mindset of lack, or doubt. You should drop this goal and focus on something else.

If the visualization makes you feel good – excited, energized, like you already have the thing – then you are on the right track.

> *"How do you keep yourself going...we got results in our heads that made us feel certain it had already happen. The secret is to get the belief to be real by seeing it enough times, and feel it enough times that our brains believe it and then it happens." - Anthony Robbins*

There are countless examples of high-performing professional athletes, business people and success gurus who stress the importance of visualization.

Michael Jordan always visualized his last shot of a game before taking it.

When Jim Carrey was a young, broke actor, he would visualize directors being interested him, and being signed to big roles. He even wrote himself a check for 10 million dollars and dated it 3 years into the future. Just 2 years later, he was offered 10 million dollars for his role in *Dumb & Dumber*.

One of the most impressive anecdotes about the power of visualization comes from the book *The Art of Learning*, by Joshua Waitzkin.

7 weeks before he was to compete in the world championships of Tai Chi Push Hands, Josh fractured one of his arms. His broken arm was put in a cast for 6 weeks, which meant that he would only have one week before the tournament to train with an arm that would certainly be weakened by muscle atrophy.

He was crushed – there was no way he could win the tournament with only one good arm.

III. Decide Where You Want to Go

But Josh didn't give up on his goal.

For 6 weeks he trained with only one arm. However, he visualized doing the same training movements with his broken arm.

Miraculously, when they took off his cast, <u>there was no muscle atrophy</u>. His broken arm looked as healthy and strong as ever – just as strong as the arm that wasn't broken.

He went on to compete in – and **win** – the world championship of Tai Chi Push Hands.

Visualize your desire in detail and visualize it often. For at least 2 minutes at a time, as often as you can throughout the day.

Through visualization your mind creates a vivid vision of reality, which then seeps into your subconscious mind. Your subconscious sees that your current reality is different from your visualized picture of reality and begins to work to correct this.

Another powerful technique is to begin verbalizing your dreams through affirmations. Say your desires out loud to yourself. Write them down every day. Repeat them to yourself like a mantra: "I am someone who travels the world making money online".

In an interview with Tim Ferriss, Scott Adams, creator of the Dilbert comic series and numerous best-sellers, attributes daily affirmations to much of his success. His technique is to write down his stated goal 15 times on a piece of paper every day.

To quote Adams: "It has never *not* worked. It has only not worked *yet* [7]."

Tell people about your dreams. Speak about it often enough and you will create a silent accountability partner of yourself. You won't want to let yourself down, or disappoint people when they ask, "so whatever happened with that amazing business idea you told me about?"

---

[7] https://tim.blog/2015/09/22/scott-adams-the-man-behind-dilbert/

Have you ever noticed that when you think often about something, you begin to see it more and more?

Try it for a few days. Start fantasizing about something that you want, like owning some flashy supercar. You will begin to see it everywhere – in magazines, on TV, in Facebook ads, on the street.

The real interesting question here is whether these actually begin to appear in the world more frequently as a result of your thoughts, or whether they were already there and you just begin noticing them more because you've changed your focus.

Traditional neuron and synapse models have postulated that our brains are capable of processing information at a rate of 1 quintillion (a one with 18 zeros!) calculations per second [8].

However this number is based on the number of neurons firing, and does not really account for our total ability to store information because we do not know how much information can be stored by a single neuron [9].

Imagine for a moment that your brain takes in all information about reality simultaneously, including everything happening at the nonphysical, subtle energetic levels.

Our conscious mind only has the computing hardware to focus on little bits of information at a time – we need to survive in the physical world, so we mostly react to and process sensory information.

You can think of your subconscious mind as a vast storehouse that holds this nearly infinite reservoir of information and releases information to you when you need it.

This also seems to be the mechanism behind dreaming. While you sleep, your subconscious allows deeply-held impressions or information to rise to your conscious mind in the form of dreams. Hopefully you can remember the dream and interpret its meaning.

When you focus intensely on something, your subconscious will automatically begin to feed your conscious mind with relevant information, thoughts, ideas,

---

[8] https://www.scienceabc.com/humans/the-human-brain-vs-supercomputers-which-one-wins.html
[9] http://chrisfwestbury.blogspot.pt/2014/06/on-processing-speed-of-human-brain.html

III. Decide Where You Want to Go

intuitions, and small actions to take in order to make that visualization into reality. It will direct the focus of your conscious mind.

Visualization, goal-setting, affirmations and mantras all work to the same end – they "program" the subconscious.

The best thing about the subconscious is that once it has been programmed, it works on auto-pilot to coordinate all the energies and circumstances that you need to take action on.

It is an obedient cybernetic slave. It will respond directly to the programming you give it.

This programming needs to be given in the form of a positive, because the mind does not understand negations.

For instance, if I say to you now, "Do not think about a pink elephant", what happens?

You probably have a pink elephant dancing around your head now.

Your mind only responds to sensory input or emotion and not the negative command. This is a crucial point.

If you give your mind the instruction, "I do not want any more micromanaging bosses", your subconscious will only understand the instruction: "micromanaging bosses", and look for more of that.

So before you begin the visualization make sure that your goals are <u>always constructed in the positive</u>. Your goals should answer the question: "What do I want?" and not "What don't I want?"

The programming also needs to be consistent. This is why sending a counter-intention negates the process.

If you lack belief, you are effectively sending one instruction in the form of a desire, then the opposite instruction in the form of a worry. They cancel each other out and the subconscious doesn't move toward your goal.

This brings us to Step 2.

Step Two: Allowing

This is by far the most difficult step, and the one we will devote the most time to addressing.

It is easy to ask for something. We are doing it all the time.

Step two is the crossroads where our dreams manifest – or die.

This is where we struggle the most. It's a battleground where a war is continuously fought between two energetic forces.

Fighting out of the red corner! A force for good, positive vibrations and dreams. The steward of human greatness. The eternal defending champion of success and progress. The spirit animal. The muse. The Buddha. The one... the only...

Allowing!

Fighting out of the blue corner! A being created of pure cunning and malevolence. The merciless obstacle to all human potential. The saboteur of spirit. The poisoned well, Lucifer, the Demented One. That horrible prince of despair...

Resistance!

The two primary ways we resist the manifestation of our desires have already been named:

Worry and Self-Doubt.

When you worry or are anxious about something, you are in fact projecting the worst possible future outcome and acting as if that will happen. Instead of asking for a dream, you are signaling for a nightmare.

Now I am not suggesting that you freak out every time you catch yourself worrying. It's completely normal and human to worry from time to time. And as long as you are feeling good and confidently projecting your vibration most of the time, you needn't worry about worry.

But when worry becomes the dominant emotion, it's time to readjust. You should either focus on a new goal that causes less worry, or employ techniques that reduce or eliminate worry.

Self-doubt is a harder beast to slay, and it's one that most of us can never really finish off. Even the most successful people deal with occasional self-doubt, the fear of not being good or deserving enough, or of being "found out" to be a fraud.

Again, it is normal to engage in occasional self-doubt, but it should only represent a dip in your emotional state to balance off the peaks of euphoria. If self-doubt becomes your default state then you need to mitigate this, as it could stem from a deep wound from your past which still troubles you. This level of self-doubt can be overcome by re-calibrating your goals to something that feels more attainable – something higher on the "belief scale".

We can mitigate worry and self-doubt through mindfulness practices: yoga, breath work and meditation.

Meditation does not only mean sitting quietly in a chair and trying not to think (that is impossible anyway).

You can substitute for the word meditation the practice that suits you.

Running can be meditation.

So can swimming, cooking, washing dishes, walking, lifting heavy weights, or hiking.

Meditation is *state*, not a practice. It is a term for the state in which you become detached from your thoughts and emotions and the mind becomes silent. You focus your attention on just one thing and your mind turns inward. You become balanced and experience the peace of being present.

Meditation allows you to go beyond your thoughts. You realize that your thoughts are not a part of you – you can choose not to identify with them. You can choose not to react to them. You can simply watch them. You become the observer.

With practice you can begin to experience peace in the now. You accept the unfolding. You allow.

You must have heard or read about how many of the successful people in this world practice meditation.

I believe that this is the primary reason – to combat worry and self-doubt. To keep your internal house in order.

When you undertake any entrepreneurial endeavor or otherwise jump into murky and uncharted waters, the thrill of "quitting" will eventually wear off and you will be faced with great uncertainty.

You've left the comfort of your cushy job with a guaranteed monthly salary for the completely unknown. You aren't sure how you will support yourself. You will experience moments in which you will feel like you don't deserve your dream. You will feel like you aren't good enough, you're stupid, you've made a terrible error in judgment.

Worry, anxiety and crushing self-doubt will creep in.

Mindfulness practices will help you cope with all that.

The Time Lag

Allowing is the period of time in between the setting of your intention and its manifestation.

There is always a time lag. Your dream, unless it is very small, will typically not manifest itself immediately. The bigger the dream, typically the longer the time lag.

This time is a hidden pitfall, perhaps more devious and relentless than the others.

A lot of goal-setting advice says to put a time limit on your goals. For instance, you want 1,000 Facebook likes for your business page by a certain date.

Or you want to achieve X monthly salary in 3 years.

Setting a time limit can be effective at generating motivation for your goals and keeping yourself accountable to your actions.

However, attempting to set deadlines on your dreams can also contain within it the seeds of defeat.

If a certain amount of time has gone by and your dream still hasn't materialized, you may begin to doubt yourself because it hasn't come in yet, and this is counterproductive.

You may cause yourself undue stress and anxiety, which can be detrimental to your health and well-being. It is difficult to feel a sense of contentedness and peace with an arbitrary deadline looming.

What is the point of chasing your goal if you feel miserable along the way?

What happens if the deadline arrives and your wish hasn't materialized? Does that mean you've failed? Do you give up then?

Time is a completely arbitrary human construct.

Visualize for a moment a world in which there are no humans – only plants and animals.

There are no meetings, no Mondays, no birthdays.

What is time then?

Lifting heavy shit, yoga, breathwork and meditation are what makes it all work for me.

It keeps me in a state of allowing and presence, largely free from worry. It is an antidote against the impatience I sometimes feel during the time lag.

Allow yourself to fall into the unfolding of your dreams. Cherish the small moments. Celebrate the small victories.

For long periods of time it can seem like nothing is happening, but all of the small actions you are taking are building momentum. The invisible energies shaping your desire are gathering forces on the sidelines. They may be outside of your conscious awareness but they are making things happen for you.

Love and enjoy the process. Results will come. Money will come.

If you focus only on the results you will not enjoy the process. 99% of our human experience is the process. The results come and you will feel a sense of achievement, and feeling accomplished is one of the nicest feelings in the world and certainly one that we should continue to strive for.

But this feeling is transient.

Your feeling of satisfaction and achievement will fade, a new goal will quickly take its place, and with that a new process toward that goal.

If you are unable to enjoy the process, most of your life will be miserable.

Enjoy the unfolding. Get out of your own way. Allow your reality to manifest on its own time.

There is a nonphysical intelligence coordinating all things, and it is infinitely smarter than you are.

There is no need to rush about. You don't know when the best time might be for something to happen. Everything will happen for you when it needs to.

This is allowing.

Step Three: Receiving

This last step is the simplest.

There is nothing more to do.

You have allowed your request to be granted, and now you receive it.

Enjoy its manifestation and appreciate it before moving onto your next desire.

III. Decide Where You Want to Go

The 3-Day Process

I learned about this concept from Bentinho Massaro and his Trinfinity Academy.

Bentinho explains an important nuance to the 3-step manifestation process which he calls the 3-Day Process.

The 3-Day Process is a complementary model to the 3-Step Process. It doesn't refer to 3 actual days, but the 3 necessary steps of manifestation which may occur across an indeterminate length of time.

Day 1 and Day 3 are the same as Steps 1 and 3 from above. On Day 1 you send out your intention or desire into the universe, and on Day 3 you receive it.

Day 2 is where the nuance lies and this occurs during Step 2: Allowing.

During Day 2, the universe will respond to your Asking by testing you. It will present an opportunity or circumstance to you that is somehow in opposition to what you really want; it will be something that masterfully plays on your fears and self-doubts.

It could be that malicious entity known as Resistance.

Or it could simply be your subconscious or True Self trying to protect you – by doing so it asks you, "are you sure you really want this?"

Either way, it is a rule. Expect it to happen.

I can best relate this concept with one of my own anecdotes.

As I discussed in the beginning of this book, some years ago I had become miserable in the high-flying consulting job I once enjoyed. I was thinking of quitting and spending some time in another country before looking for work in another area of industry that I became interested in.

I had a meeting scheduled with my boss. I was determined to quit.

The evening before the day of the meeting, I received a call from a headhunter. It was a person I had spoken with before, but had not heard from in at least a year.

III. Decide Where You Want to Go

He asked me how I was doing. I told him what I was planning to do the next day. He said that he had not seen any jobs for me lately. Then he wished me well.

That was it? He called me just to say that there were no jobs?

It was odd.

But my fears crept in – I began to doubt my decision to quit. Maybe I should hold onto my job after all, I thought. It was a good job and I was lucky to have it.

The strangeness of the interaction and its timing did make me think that it might be a test of sorts, but it filled me with enough doubt that I couldn't follow through with my plan the next day. I got scared; I took a half-measure. Instead of quitting, I asked to reduce my hours to part time.

My boss agreed to this in principle but I doubted that it would actually happen. Most of the colleagues I had known who tried to reduce to part time ended up still working full time but with a part time salary. And we had just won a massive new client and would be understaffed even if I continued working full time.

A few months went by.

I was still miserable; even more miserable than before. Nothing had changed. I had not really decided anything. My wife had recently launched her own company and was completely dependent on me financially. I felt trapped by the responsibility.

But this time I was <u>really</u> determined to quit. I had my wife's full support. She was tired of seeing me unhappy.

Again I had scheduled a meeting with my boss to tell him about my plans. I would work until a certain date, then take at least 3 months off and move to Berlin.

The evening before the day of this meeting, my phone rang.

It was the same headhunter from last time.

He asked me how I was doing. I told him my plans. Again, he told me that there were no jobs, and wished me well.

I had not communicated with him since the previous time he had called. I have not spoken to him ever again since.

III. Decide Where You Want to Go

This was too much of a coincidence to be anything other than a test.

From my study of depth psychology and archetypes I realized that the headhunter represented the negative aspect of the archetypal father. That is the part of me – the part of all of us – where fear of the unknown resides. The part that desires stability, security and comfort. The part that is rational, logical, grounded, dependable, and steady. The practical, sensible one that wants to protect you. The provider.

This was Day 2. The test. It played on all of the above emotions and fears.

But this time I identified it for what it was. I decided to ignore its advice.

The next day I met with my boss and announced to him I was going to quit and go to Berlin. I would not be seeking a leave of absence.

Two weeks after I made this decision, my wife suddenly began making money – enough to support herself.

I spent the last few months on the job enjoying myself immensely.

If you've never quit a job you've hated before, I highly recommend it. It's one of the best feelings there is.

At some point shortly before leaving – as a result of some small action that I had taken which I had promptly forgotten about – I received a call from a recruiter about a job at a different company in precisely the area of industry that I wanted to explore.

I went through the whole interview process and received a job offer from this new company which was finalized the same week I left for Berlin. A CHF 15,000 annual salary increase, more benefits, better bonus scheme, and fewer working hours. I told them that I was going to Berlin for 3 months. They said they would wait for me.

I could leave for Berlin with complete peace of mind, knowing that I had a new and exciting job waiting for me when I got back.

It was exactly what I wanted.

And all because I believed that I could get exactly what I wanted, and correctly recognized Day 2 for what it was and continued forward.

III. Decide Where You Want to Go

Action

The second key thing to manifesting your desires is to take action.

The Secret does not say much about actions. You could read the book and come away thinking that no action is necessary. Just think and wait, and your desires will magically appear before you.

Your thoughts and emotions *do* need to come first. You must regulate your thoughts, experience positive emotions and expect great things for yourself.

Tend to your mind as if it were your own personal garden and your life absolutely depended on the fruits it bears. Work on your mindset and your thinking harder than at anything else.

And you should visualize what you want in detail.

But actual results come from action.

It's ultimately the actions that create the circumstances, people and events that will move you along the path to your ultimate destination. And when circumstances present themselves, you must take action.

You needn't worry too much about which actions you should take. If your mind is right and you feel good – whatever "good" means for you right now – your actions will seem natural, effortless.

Your thoughts will create the emotions that lead to the corresponding action, which will give you results and a new set of circumstances.

So you can go ahead and visualize checks coming to you the mail.

But in the first instance, you must truly believe that it is possible for checks to come to you in the mail. If you believe it is possible and it excites you, you will naturally begin to take little actions in the direction of making this mental movie into reality.

In Rhonda Byrne's case, she took the actions of writing books and producing a movie about *The Secret*, which generated plenty of royalty checks to her in the mail.

She took massive action to make that happen – she wrote four books and had a movie produced.

III. Decide Where You Want to Go

"But I don't know which actions to take!"

Do not worry about this. Really!

I cannot stress this enough. If you are focused on what you want and doing everything you can to make yourself feel good, the right circumstances will present themselves. You will know what you need to do. The right teachers will appear. Useful feedback will guide you.

Taking my example from the last section. I took a small action which a recruiter picked up on, which led to further actions that I took and landed myself a better job. I did things. But the things felt so smooth and natural. It was effortless. And I knew it was the right thing at the time because I felt great about it. I felt 100% congruent with everything that was happening.

III. Decide Where You Want to Go

Principle #1: Feel Good Now

Here is the real *Secret*.

No matter what your goal is, you should spend the majority of your time managing your thoughts and emotions with the aim of feeling as good as possible.

Below are some specific things you can do to feel good and be in a state of positive expectation as often as possible:

- → Go for long walks in nature
- → Exercise, play a sport, lift weights
- → Eat natural foods – greens, vegetables, fresh fruit, farm-raised meats, wild caught fish
- → Take vitamin and mineral supplements
- → Get a pet, or play with your pet
- → Take a sauna or go for a steam
- → Meditate
- → Do yoga
- → Take cold showers
- → Get a massage
- → Listen to music
- → Play a musical instrument
- → Dance
- → Sing
- → Call someone you love

This is by no means an exhaustive list and I encourage you to find your own ways to feel good.

Make sure it is something that you can do regularly. Ideally you will spend at least 30 minutes of every day doing something that makes you feel good.

Your future is created from the seeds of now. Feel good now, feel good later.

III. Decide Where You Want to Go

Principle #2: Monitor Your Emotions

As you continue working on feeling good and following your desires, things will begin to come into your experience: new people, opportunities, activities, and chances to grow. You will need to take action.

The trick when taking action is to pay very, very careful attention to your emotions.

Remember that you are mostly energy, a vibrational being. Your emotions are your guide through life. They are your own personal GPS system and they will tell you when you are off track.

Your excitement, your bliss, are like breadcrumbs on your path in life.

You know the story of Hansel and Gretel, those two kids who left breadcrumbs as they traveled through the witch's forest to remember their path back. Your feeling of bliss is just like this, except they represent breadcrumbs indicating your path *forward* in life.

<u>Always</u> follow your bliss!

So when an opportunity comes and you are deliberating which action to take, get out of your head and listen to your emotions. How do you **feel** about doing it? Is it in line with your values? Do you have any doubts about it?

You will know you are on the right track when you have a feeling of congruence. Feeling congruent is like feeling you are in a "flow" state – your emotions, mind, body, values and goals are 100% aligned with your actions.

You will know the feeling when it hits you. Listen to your gut.

When you are fully congruent, everything will feel effortless – the action will feel like the most natural thing in the world to do. It will fill you with an inner smile. It will excite you and challenge you. You will feel at peace.

If you feel bad about something – if it causes anger or frustration, violates your values or your integrity – then you are not in a state of congruence and you shouldn't do it.

For many of us, this will take some practice.

III. Decide Where You Want to Go

We are used to living in our heads, and switching to a state of emotional awareness will take some getting used to. But if you are regularly using the "feel good" techniques listed in the previous section, it will become much easier with time.

III. Decide Where You Want to Go

Principle #3: Cultivate Awareness

Cultivating greater self-awareness isn't really something that can be "taught".

Being "aware" is parallel to being present and monitoring your emotions. Every person, every event, every interaction and circumstance in your life contains a message. This message is custom-tailored for your unique path in life.

You can think of it as the universe itself giving you energetic feedback through its various forms.

Every person has something to teach you. Every person is better than you in some way. Each interaction can be significant. If you are present and paying attention, you will see this and learn. If you are not present, and off into your own thoughts and worries over the future, you may miss it.

If you react with a strong emotion to something a person said, or a specific circumstance, examine that emotion carefully.

What is it trying to communicate to you? Is there something wrong in your thinking? Is one of your fears, worries or doubts being triggered?

Who do you hate? Who do you envy?

Hate and envy will teach you a lot about yourself.

Your hate for someone could be triggering a core value that has been violated. It will also indicate the way in which you judge others, or judge yourself.

Envy is one of the most useful negative emotions. It simultaneously indicates to you something that you want, and highlights any self-doubt and feelings of "not being good enough" to have it.

Be present with whatever emotion you experience. Do not try to distract yourself or bury it. But also be careful not to wallow in it – you want to avoid the trap of self-pity and self-victimization.

Let's say you applied to a job and didn't receive the decision you wanted. This may give rise to unpleasant emotions, and these emotions will indicate to you how passionate you were toward achieving that particular goal. You will gain more feedback as to what worked and what didn't, and you can use this to fine tune your approach.

Cultivating awareness is almost like developing a sixth sense. It is a very deep sort of listening – to yourself, to circumstances, and to people. Be present with everything.

How do you train awareness?

The first step is Self-knowledge. By now, if you have done the exercises in this book, you should have some clarity as to what you're all about: your values, beliefs, dreams and goals.

The rest of the training comes with mindfulness and practice using these techniques. Meditation (or whichever mindfulness technique you prefer) will assist you in being in the Now. It takes time and practice, so be patient – it may take years before you have fine-tuned your awareness enough to interpret the feedback. You will begin to observe coincidences and understand them for what they are: feedback for your present intention.

III. Decide Where You Want to Go

Goal-Setting

We've spent a lot of time talking about setting goals in order to get specific things that you want.

Almost all the goal-setting gurus say the same thing: know exactly what you want and be super, hyper-specific about your goals.

For instance, instead of saying that you want to "make a million dollars in some business", you should state your goal as follows:

> "I want to make a million dollars annual revenue in a limited partnership company making sustainably-sourced supplement products for the North American market in partnership with Onnit Labs, and I will achieve this by November 12th, 20XX."

Or, instead of saying that you want to become a best-selling author, you should say:

> "I will make the #1 Bestselling list of the New York Times in the genre of historical non-fiction by the time I turn 30. My book will have written endorsements from Niall Ferguson and David McCullough. I will launch my book-signing tour after my appearance on the Oprah Winfrey show."

Then you take your goal and break it down into monthly, weekly, even daily targets. Treat yourself like a business.

The idea here is that only by being hyper-specific about your goals will you be able to filter out the appropriate actions necessary to getting there and be able to measure your progress.

There is a ton of merit to this strategy, and there is no question that it works. If you already know your goal to such detail then it is to your advantage to make it as specific as possible.

However, there is one major drawback to this approach:

What if *you don't know* your goal in such detail?

What if your dreams are more of a general nature?

III. Decide Where You Want to Go

What if you want to experience more fun, adventure, and happiness? How do you set measurable daily targets for that? It's possible, only harder and more frustrating to pin down.

If you take the commonly-given advice of being hyper specific, you may become paralyzed. Out of uncertainty of not knowing exactly what you want, you will do nothing. You will hesitate. You will stall.

This is the biggest trap with the idea of "finding your passion". People have this idea that they need to find their Passion, their One and Only Thing that They Are Meant to Do.

This is nonsense, and it isn't the case for the vast majority of people.

Passions change throughout life. If you wait around to find that one before taking action, you won't do anything.

III. Decide Where You Want to Go

Find out your true goal

Right now you might have all sorts of goals in your mind:

New car. Better job. Bigger salary. Private jet. Become famous on YouTube. Mansion on the beach. Passive income.

Whatever it is, now I want you to ask yourself: "What does this goal really mean for me?"

At the core of each goal is a feeling. The material goal only represents a certain feeling that you want to have.

For instance if you are seeking a huge promotion, what you really want is the feeling of being significant, important, powerful, or having the freedom and increased living standards that an increased salary will afford you.

If your goal is to travel the world while making passive income, what you really want is to feel a sense of freedom and adventure.

If you want to be famous, what you really want is to be loved, respected, admired, and receive attention (probably from your daddy, but that's for another discussion).

Goals Exercise:

Go through your list of goals again. For each goal, answer the question: "Why do I really want this goal? What feeling will I get when I have this? Which of my needs are being fulfilled?"

See if several of your goals relate to a similar feeling or unmet need.

That feeling or need is your true goal.

Focus on the feeling

This is the approach I personally take: I focus on the feeling I want to have.

Your desired feeling will naturally change over time as your life situation changes.

For example it could mean feeling:

- → Contentedness
- → Joy
- → Excitement
- → Bliss
- → Love
- → Passion
- → Power
- → Admiration
- → Spiritual growth
- → Inspired
- → Connected
- → Comfortable
- → Security
- → Purpose

What do you want to feel now? What has been lacking in your life?

Your answer will indicate to you the primary feeling you want to have. It could also be a combination of several feelings.

If you've been dealing with a lot of turmoil and uncertainty, maybe stability is the thing for you.

Perhaps you're feeling bored and could use some more passion and excitement in life.

III. Decide Where You Want to Go

Or you've felt unconnected to others, and what you really need now is greater love and connection.

It can change from month to month, week to week or even day to day. Monitor your emotions and calibrate as needed.

Let's say you want to focus on feeling joy. What does it actually feel like in your body?

Remember a time that you felt really joyful, and visualize it in detail. Put yourself in the moment. See the sights, hear the sounds. Are certain areas of your body activated? What is your posture like? What thoughts are you thinking?

Once you know how joy feels in your body, you can re-create that feeling anytime you want.

Then, your external goals fade in importance. You've already achieved the desired state. Your surroundings will then begin to change to match your internal state. Your internal state is the "lens" through which you interpret the world.

It's simple. But not easy. We forget – we become entangled with our environment and lose perspective of cause and effect.

Remember: the inner creates the outer. The outer can only reinforce what is inside.

Is being hyper-specific and disciplined with your goals faster? Sure.

But what's the rush?

Who are you racing against?

Take it easy. Slow down. Smell the roses. Enjoy life.

You can race if you want, but remember that the race doesn't end.

It's never enough. You'll always want more: more money, more Instagram followers, more stuff.

Just focus on the feeling, and allow the unfolding.

But what do I do if I'm completely miserable?

There are a number of exercises you can do to raise your emotional state. The book *Ask and It is Given* by Jerry and Esther Hicks contains dozens of techniques for raising your emotional state – you definitely want to have this book in your toolkit.

One simple and indispensable technique is Appreciation.

All happy people have this in common. <u>All</u> of them.

They have a daily practice of being grateful for what they have.

No matter your situation in life, you have **something** that you can be grateful for. The simple fact that you are able to read these words means you have the gift of sight. Not everyone does.

Then you can probably be grateful that your arms and legs function. That you're breathing and that your heart beats for you without asking for anything in return. That you are alive and able to experience the mystery of existing on this blue pearl adrift in the unfathomable vastness of the universe. That you have a brain and a consciousness which is capable of pondering such questions. That you are conscious of the fact that you are conscious.

The last paragraph is an example of a Rampage of Appreciation.

You begin by appreciating one thing, and that leads to another thought and another thing you can be appreciative of. If you practice this for just a couple of minutes you will notice a huge shift in your emotional state toward a feeling of gratitude and being blessed.

Instantly, your vibrational state has increased from one of feeling disempowered, to one of feeling grateful and entering into a state of Allowing.

III. Decide Where You Want to Go

Why general goals are better than specific ones

I believe that there is an energetic intelligence at work in the universe.

Whether you want to call it God, Buddha, energy, Universe, or cosmic universal consciousness, it does not matter.

We are all somehow connected to everything else around us, and the nearly infinite number of interrelated energetic variables that interact continuously to form what we perceive as reality, evolution, or creation.

Both Western and Eastern spiritual traditions agree in one aspect: normal human consciousness is not the ultimate tier of Being.

Western religions teach that there is one omnipotent God. Eastern traditions believe in many gods, or no god but a universal cosmic intelligence or consciousness of which all things are a part.

In my view they are simply different expressions of the same thing – a higher energetic state that exists at a higher plane of consciousness or nonphysical dimension.

This intelligence is energetic in nature. It knows you infinitely better than you know yourself, because your True Self – your highest consciousness – is an inseparable part of that intelligence.

This means that the intelligence will provide you with better results if you let it work for you.

You're not smart enough to know everything that needs to happen to you on your personal life journey.

You can set specific goals and "muscle" your way through them. Definitely, it works.

When you focus on the feelings, you let the intelligence, the Universe handle the details for you, and in the end you get better stuff.

This is Allowing in its purest sense.

However it is worth emphasizing that the Universe does not play favorites. It does not care about you. It only responds in kind to the energy that you resonate.

III. Decide Where You Want to Go

If you are brimming with positivity, confidence, belief in yourself, living in joy and expect miracles for yourself, you will experience more joy and miracles.

If you think that the world is out to get you, that life has and always will be unfair to you, that there is no point trying because these things are for the 1%– then you will experience circumstances that give you more of the same.

What if I make the wrong choice?

Some people might be wondering:

> Okay, now what? I have my dreams, I am doing my visualization, I am practicing awareness. I am a curious person and am being pulled in many different directions and I don't know what I should choose.

We are inundated by choice, and are being presented with questions that historically we didn't have the luxury of asking, such as:

Which country should I live in?

What should I study?

Which career should I pursue?

When you are inundated by choice, you have the problem of "buyer's remorse".

It has been shown that when people have more choice, they are less happy. If you have 100 different cereals to choose from, that means that there are 99 cereals that could have potentially been better than the one you chose. If there are only 2 types of cereal, you won't feel as much regret after purchase.

The same applies to life choices, and can make it difficult to fully commit to anything. You may be interested in many things, but you only have one life, and you cannot do everything – so what do you choose?

Know that there is no "wrong choice".

Just start doing something. Anything. Start somewhere.

Did you have the idea to start a podcast? Start asking your friends if they want to do a podcast with you.

Do you dream of being a writer? Start writing.

Do you want to be a digital nomad? Begin researching and looking for a community of nomads that you would like to join.

Don't know which type of job you want? Just get a job, any job, or change your job. Then discover what you like or don't like about it.

The specific actions really do not matter at this stage.

III. Decide Where You Want to Go

The point is for you to take any action. Take big actions, small actions, many different actions.

It's like throwing different batches of dough against a kitchen wall. See which activity sticks.

Which activity do you enjoy the most?

Which activities are you still doing 6 months later, and what do they have in common?

A few years ago I went through this same phase. I began keeping a blog. I started a podcast. I joined startup communities to see what they were doing. I practiced public speaking. And so on.

I ended up dropping some of these activities, but they were all useful. Through my first short-lived attempt at a podcast I ended up speaking with people doing inspiring things, and this gave me ideas. Those ideas evolved and contributed in a major way to the life I am living now.

Through my short stint assisting a startup, I got to see how a different community operated and was further able to refine my preferences.

When it comes to reinventing yourself, there is no such thing as wasted actions. You are here to have a human experience. You are growing, evolving, and there is no hurry.

Every experience is good in that it gives you valuable feedback.

Do I like this? What do I like about this? What don't I like about this?

What do I want more of, and why?

Life is simply a journey of incrementally refining your preferences.

IV.
The Journey Ahead

> "Resistance is not a peripheral opponent. Resistance arises from within. It is self-generated and self-perpetuated. Resistance is the enemy within" - Steven Pressfield, The War of Art

A difficult path lies ahead of you.

It is never easy to leave behind something that you have grown comfortable with, and begin asking yourself the difficult questions.

Who am I really?

What kind of person am I?

What kind of life do I want?

How can I best serve others?

How can I add the most value to the world?

Most people identify strongly with the static forms of their lives: their job, their community, their relationships, the culture in which they live.

When you suddenly take all that away, you may experience an identity crisis.

When I went through this process, sometimes I felt totally lost, like I was in Purgatory.

On the worst days, I have questioned _everything_. Down to the fundamental levels. Who the hell was I? Was I a complete loser that just couldn't hold down a job? I reflected on my past and wondered if I was a terrible person. I questioned my 10-year relationship with my wife.

IV. The Journey Ahead

One day I went into the grocery store and was struck by a mild panic attack. I had to buy snacks for an event at the coworking space where I was working and simply could not make a decision. I was overwhelmed by the choices. Then I lost the piece of paper with our account number on it. I was going to be late to the event and it would be ruined. I dropped a cherry tomato, then nearly tripped over an old lady trying to pick it up.

I stumbled out of the store. I couldn't do anything right. Couldn't hold a job; couldn't even fucking buy snacks. My heart raced and I began to panic.

It was a microcosm for where I felt in life; directionless and without a clear path forward.

This is the road less traveled. You may find yourself without guidance or example to follow.

Expect this sort of thing to happen and you will be better equipped for the challenges ahead.

Here is what your emotional curve will look like after you've embarked on your journey:

Somehow, however confident I felt the previous day, no matter how much work I had done or how optimistic I had been, getting up in the morning was a daily struggle.

Lying in bed as the faint morning light trickled in behind the curtains, my barely wakeful consciousness began to activate. My first thoughts of the day were plagued by self-doubt and fear. Getting out of bed felt like an enormous effort, a monumental struggle against inertia, and it seemed much simpler to continue delaying the start of my day as long as possible.

The tasks before me seemed insurmountable. I wasn't good enough. Why should anyone listen to what I have to say? The market was already too crowded. I was a fraud.

The urge to reach for my phone and lie in bed for another hour consuming social media or news was too tempting.

This was Resistance.

But, why?

Did I have horrible, tormenting dreams and not remember them? How could I go from feeling capable of doing nearly anything after a highly productive day of Doing the Work, to a self-doubting mess that didn't want to get out of bed in the space of 7 hours?

The sleep state of consciousness seemed to be a great eraser. Each day my mental state was being born anew, and the default state was one of lethargy, doubt and inaction.

There was no way. Resistance was the default state.

Yoga philosophy categorizes Sleep as one of the five *vritti*, or fluctuations of the mind.

During sleep we lose control of our consciousness. The mind becomes untethered to roam at the depths of its choosing, taking painful memories and disguising them in new clothes and a strange dream context. If the dream is vivid enough that you remember it, undoubtedly it could stay with you in waking and disturb your mind.

This made sense enough.

But I have begun to think of sleep as a reset button for your consciousness, and that perhaps the ancient Yogis understood this.

During these 8 hours you are no longer yourself. Your waking consciousness and all that you identify with shuts down. You become something else, some

IV. The Journey Ahead

meandering unconsciousness that goes where it will and – unless you master the subtle art of Lucid Dreaming – you are powerless to control it.

Do we go somewhere else during sleep? Does our consciousness wander off into a different dimension full of alien energies and malevolent beings that hijack our consciousness, and send us back into the waking world in a state of self-doubt?

I didn't know, and I still don't know. But we can anticipate this and take measures against it.

Your biggest enemy is lack of structure

You are used to structure.

When you have a place to be every day, specific timelines to follow, and a set time to get from A to B, you are efficient. Effective.

Having a job is a transaction of time for money at an agreed price. Your free time is scarce, therefore more valuable, so you make the most of what little of it you have. The Man has you from 9 to 5, so you do what you can to feel free in the mornings, evenings and weekends.

Time as a human construct only serves the function of organizing our day.

Then you quit and suddenly you find yourself utterly without structure. You have nothing but time. And it has no value at first because no one is paying you for it.

When you have nowhere specific to be, time just fills up all empty space. Like a probability wave, the time function breaks down and the probability that it is wasted multiplies exponentially.

Having this much freedom of time can be surprisingly difficult to manage.

The vastness of choice is overwhelming. What should you focus your time on? Where should you go today? Should you go to a networking event or should you do some work? What about that meditation retreat you've always wanted to go on?

IV. The Journey Ahead

It starts with getting up right

We now understand that:
- → Our consciousness is "re-born" each morning;
- → Resistance/doubt/lethargy may be the default state upon waking; and
- → We need some kind of structure

The <u>good news</u> is that it actually doesn't take much time or effort to overcome this state and get back on track to being happy, confident and productive.

First, set an alarm. No later than 8.30 am.

The legendary Zig Ziglar had a simple trick to reclaim your mind from Resistance in the morning:

After your alarm goes off, you sit up tall in bed, and sing to yourself "This is a beautiful day!" 3 times while clapping your hands. Then you extend both of your arms up overhead in a celebratory pose, cheer for yourself, and jump out of bed.

It sounds silly, but it's very effective.

There are plenty of interviews in print or online about the morning routines of successful people. Do your own research. The key is just to find a routine that makes you feel good and fills you with positive energy, and is something easy and short that you can stick with long enough – everyday for 30 days – so that it becomes a habit.

Once it becomes your habit, you can look into making longer and more elaborate ways to start your day. So start with something small – 20 minutes of meditation or a morning run.

For me, it's exercise, breathwork, meditation and a cold shower.

If I can manage to get out of bed within 10 minutes and get on my yoga mat, I've won.

Any kind of exercise works. Sometimes it's heavy lifting, other days it's running or yoga. Mix it up so you don't get bored.

The one thing that never changes is the cold shower.

For me, this is absolutely key. There are hundreds of blogs and articles dedicated to describing the benefits of cold water therapy.

Yogis have been practicing a form of this therapy – called *Ishnaan* – for centuries.

Wim Hof has built an entire career out of cold therapy and it is thanks to him that I have picked it up as a habit for myself.

Cold showers have been shown to boost immune function, improve skin tone, reduce inflammation and lower blood pressure.

Importantly, it has been shown to have positive effects on mood. This is the main benefit it brings me.

Like jumping out of bed when your alarm goes off, it's hard to do. You just have to turn the shower knob to the max, grit your teeth and get through it.

But like most things, it's not as bad as your mind makes it out to be, and afterward you will feel totally invigorated and energized to go out there and crush it.

I've noticed that when I don't follow my morning routine, I am 100% more likely to be lazy.

If I am able to wake up early, exercise, and take a cold shower, I already have had three small victories that day. I've already done three hard things. This gives me a boost of confidence and creates a snowball effect such that the big goals that previously seemed insurmountable become possible.

The Big Goal can then be taken on by reducing it to a series of small actions to take, much like the actions I've already completed this morning.

IV. The Journey Ahead

Follow-through is everything

Now for the real challenge.

We know that our mind tends to start off infected by Resistance.

And we know that it is important to have a good morning routine.

But waking up and exercising is hard. Cold showers are hard. Picking up a new habit requires dedication, discipline and accountability.

How do we keep it up?

First, you should remind yourself of your "why".

Go back to the list of things you wrote down in the previous chapters. Reconnect with your powerful sense of Why for that (or those) particular goal(s).

Commit to yourself. Tell yourself you will do whatever is necessary to make this happen. That you can't NOT do it.

Some people function in terms of escaping a negative rather than seeking a positive. If you are more the type of person that thinks in terms of escaping the negative (*getting away from* a bad job, *away from* a bad relationship), then remember that doing nothing is the same as asking for more of the thing that you do not want. That by NOT pursuing your goal, you are staying where you are. This is the law of inertia at work, and the same reason why it is easier to stay in bed longer each morning.

Once you build yourself up to the idea that you can't NOT do this thing – then you need to make sure you start your day off right, because it will be a long and challenging road and you will need to be at your peak of resourcefulness and mental faculty to be productive and stick it through.

Otherwise, you might end up right back where you are now.

A good morning routine is the catalyst for literally everything else that follows for the rest of the day.

A good morning routine translates directly into concrete action, and absent such action your dream or goal will remain in the domain of Imagination.

In fact, earlier in the morning before I wrote this section of the book, I was lying in bed thinking how nice it would be just to lie around, play on my phone and watch YouTube videos. I didn't set an alarm, which was my first mistake.

On this particular day, I fought through it. I put my phone down and crawled onto my yoga mat, did my meditation, took my cold shower, and then sat down to write 2,000 of the words you are now reading.

I remembered my Why; I knew both what I wanted and what I didn't want, and this is what helped translate thought into action.

In addition to remembering your Why, here are some more tips:

→ *Set your alarm early and make a commitment to yourself to wake up when it goes off*

No snoozing allowed! Develop a "penalty" for yourself each time you hit the snooze button.

It could be a random act of kindness – for instance, each time you snooze you need to pay for the Starbucks of a person in line behind you.

You could bake cookies for a friend.

Or, each snooze could translate into 1 hour of volunteering or 20 USD equivalent that you will donate to a cause that you believe in.

The ideal penalty is something that incurs a cost to you but can still benefit someone else.

The hardest part is simply getting out of bed, so pick a penalty that is appropriate to the benefit of following through.

→ *Tell your friends, family and/or partner about your new habits*

This will make you accountable to them. Ask them to give you shit if you don't do it.

Having a group of people around to hold you accountable is one of the keys to following through on anything. Ask them to check up with you from time to time to see if you are following through.

Ideally it is someone you admire, that you won't want to disappoint.

→ *Schedule your day on the previous day, or for the week in advance*

On Sunday night, plan out your week.

When you wake up, Google Calendar tells you "Stretch and meditate for 20 minutes".

A half hour later Google says: "Cold shower time, don't be a pussy. There are people that live in Siberia that don't know anything else."

Organize your tasks and use whatever language that will motivate you.

You don't need to schedule too many tasks for yourself. What's the point of keeping on a super strict schedule now that you are enjoying your freedom?

Just pick two main tasks you will spend your time on: one for the morning, and one for the afternoon. And maybe a fun activity or networking event in the evening.

→ *Write down your habits and post them everywhere*

On your bathroom mirror, next to your bed, on the ceiling above your bed, a Post-it Note taped to the screen of your mobile device each night, attached to the coffee pot… everywhere and anywhere that you will see it.

In the note, remind yourself: "You know you will feel good and be productive if you just do this. This is your future self, living your dream life, imploring you to take this one simple step right now".

Think of it as giving your future self a gift. Do it now, so that you can thank yourself later.

→ *Get a coach*

If none of the above work, then it might be time to get yourself a coach.

A coach will hold you accountable to yourself, keep you on track, re-frame your progress through the wilderness, make sure you stay clear on your goals and your why, and give you that extra push toward your goals.

Research has shown that people are twice as likely to accomplish their goals if they are working with a coach, as opposed to going it alone[10].

That, my new friend, is a call to action.

Now get your shit together.

---

[10] https://instituteofcoaching.org/coaching-overview/coaching-benefits

Afterword

Once you get close to the completion of your passion project – whether it be a book, the launch of a new business, movie script – expect a near catastrophic setback (or several of them).

It is a natural law.

The Universe is going to test you to see if you've got the passion, mettle and dedication to pick up the broken pieces and carry it through to completion.

Prepare for that to happen.

It won't necessarily make it easier, but at least you'll be less surprised.

Suggested Further Reading

Below is a short selection of books I highly recommend that you read, re-read, and read again. I also suggest you read them in this order.

1. *Reinventing Organizations,* Frederic Laloux
2. *The Magic of Thinking Big,* David Schwartz
3. *See You at the Top,* Zig Ziglar
4. *The Laws of Success in 16 Lessons,* Napoleon Hill
5. *Awaken the Giant Within,* Anthony Robbins
6. *The Success Principles,* Jack Canfield
7. *Rich Dad Poor Dad,* Robert T. Kiyosaki
8. *Ask and It Is Given,* Jerry and Esther Hicks
9. *The Science of Getting Rich,* Wallace G. Wattles
10. *The War of Art,* Steven Pressfield
11. *Meditation: The Art of Ecstasy,* Osho

Visit www.kevinholtcoaching.com/resources for further resources such as video and audio courses

Appendix

Appendix

The 7 Human Needs

SECURITY

VARIETY

FEELING OF IMPORTANCE

CONNECTION/LOVE

GROWTH

SERVICE

AUTONOMY

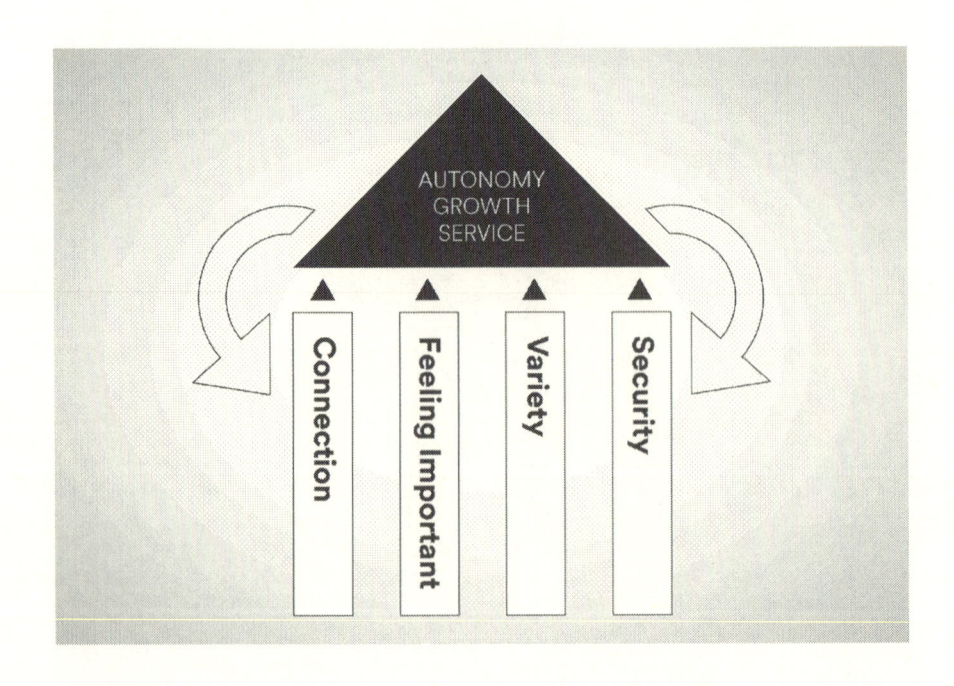

Appendix

Human Needs Worksheet #1

Need	Ranking	When do I feel that this need is met?
Security		(ex: Having a regular income)
Variety		(ex: trying a new hobby)
Feeling of Importance		(ex: my boss praises me for good work on a project)
Connection		
Growth		
Service		
Autonomy		

Human Needs Worksheet #2

Need	How do I meet this need? (Positive)	How do I need this need? (Negative)
Security		
Variety		
Feeling Important		
Connection		
Growth		
Service		
Autonomy		

Human Needs Worksheet #3

NEED	LIFE ZONE		
	My Career	**My Relationships**	**My Passion/Hobby**
Security	Steady paycheck, place to go everyday, routine	I know my loved ones will be there for me	I know I can do this, and when I practice I will enjoy it
Variety			
Feeling Important			
Connection			
Growth			
Service			
Autonomy			

Beliefs Worksheet

MY CURRENT BELIEFS		BELIEFS I WANT TO HAVE	
Global beliefs	**Personal beliefs**	**Global beliefs …[actualized]**	**Personal beliefs …[adjusted]**
You need to be smart to be financially successful.	I am not very smart.	Financial success depends more on persistence than intelligence.	Though I may not be a genius, I am reasonably smart and have common sense. I can also be hard working and persistent, which is 99% of success.

Appendix

The Model

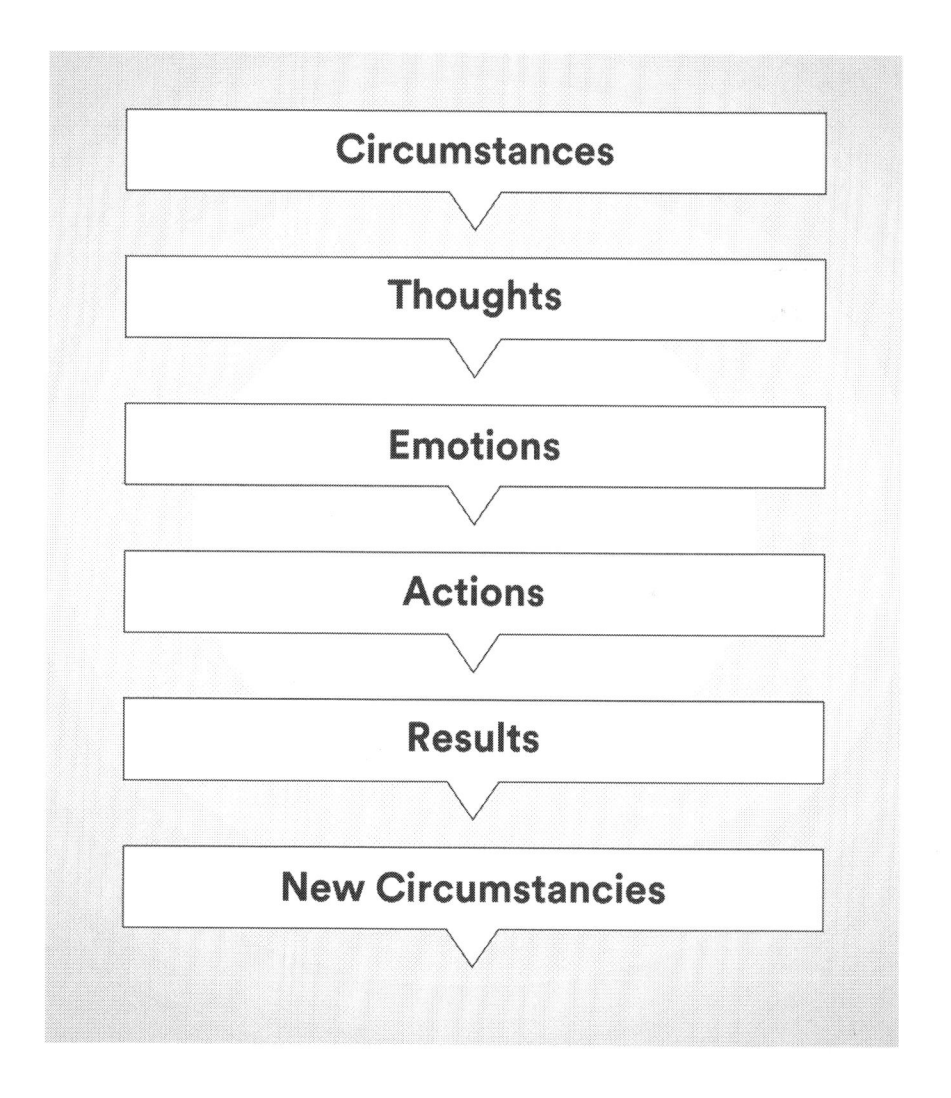

- Circumstances
- Thoughts
- Emotions
- Actions
- Results
- New Circumstancies

Notes

Made in the USA
Middletown, DE
25 August 2020